Critical Guides to French Texts

Critical Guides to French Texts

EDITED BY ROGER LITTLE, WOLFGANG VAN EMDEN, DAVID WILLIAMS

BECKETT

Molloy

Michael Sheringham

Lecturer in French
University of Kent at Canterbury

Grant & Cutler Ltd
1985

© Grant & Cutler Ltd
1985
ISBN 0 7293 0218 0

843. 91 BEC/SHE

I.S.B.N. 84-599-0409-1

DEPÓSITO LEGAL: V. 322 - 1985

Printed in Spain by
Artes Gráficas Soler, S.A., Valencia
for
GRANT & CUTLER LTD
11 BUCKINGHAM STREET, LONDON W.C.2

Contents

To my Father

Prefatory Note

Everyone knows that too much has been written about Beckett: 'more books about him than by him ... his books get shorter, the critical ones longer ... should be a moratorium ... Beckett industry ...'. And yet .... I would not have written the present study if I had not felt dissatisfied with what I had read on Beckett's fiction, and uncertain what to recommend to enthusiastic undergraduates. The principal way in which I have tried to remedy if not quell my dissatisfaction has been to stay very close to my chosen text and to treat *Molloy* as a novel above all else and not a treatise, a symptom, a stage on the author's way. This accounts for my delaying any account of the novel's genesis until the third section of chapter one, and for the predominance of running commentary in the book's central chapters. Despite what I have said I am, of course, deeply indebted to earlier commentators on Beckett's novels. But in preparing this study I also found myself repeatedly turning to and mulling over recent work in narrative theory which has given us a fuller understanding of what fictions are made of and stressed the remarkable things they can do. Both kinds of debt are reflected in the Select Bibliography at the end of this volume. I also owe much to the friends and colleagues at Kent with whom, for several years, I taught an interdisciplinary course on which Beckett figured prominently; so it is with pleasure and fond memories of some vigorous discussions that I mention Bernard Sharrat, Martin Scofield, Peter Hainsworth, Ray Gaita, Marion O'Connor, Larry Chase, Roger Cardinal, Keith Carabine and David Bradby. Finally I should like to thank Roger Little for all his help and patience.

The edition of *Molloy* referred to in this study is that published by Editions de Minuit in the Collection 'Double', 1982. Italicised numbers refer to the Select Bibliography.

1. Finding a Form

Reading *Molloy* is a dazzling but often bewildering experience. All kinds of things try to monopolise our attention: the two voluble narrators and the fuss they make telling their stories; the stories themselves with their echoes and contrasts and common core of mythic and archetypal matter; elements of the philosophical tradition at its most sublimely disinterested; elements of the comic tradition at its most coarse and scatological; much else besides. In its essentials the narrative content of the novel is relatively simple and unproblematic. Without much difficulty we can enumerate the various settings and encounters which punctuate Molloy's account of his unsuccessful quest for his mother, and Moran's account of his abortive quest for Molloy. The profusion of circumstantial detail, the blurred nature of some of the narrative transitions, the uncertainty which surrounds specific incidents and which clouds the conclusion of both narratives, as well as the relationship between them — all these obstacles can be surmounted if we are intent on making a list of the principal 'events'. There is however little to be said for trying to surmount these obstacles without taking into account the remarkable variety of factors which shape and regulate the narrative content, for it is clear that these will ultimately determine the novel's range of meaning; and the moment we do begin to try and assess these factors *Molloy*, for all the simplicity of its content, becomes a very rich and complex novel indeed.

Our initial impression of this abundance is likely to derive from four main features. Firstly, the division into two narratives, and the elaborate system of connections, cross-references, parallels, contrasts and echoes which goes with it; secondly and thirdly, the mythic, and the philosophical, overtones with which the text seems so richly loaded; fourthly, the constant emphasis on the activity of narration itself, both narrators being inclined to pronounce frequently, lengthily, and often inconsistently on such questions as where, when, and on whose behalf they are telling their stories, while also maintaining a running commentary on their own performance as narrators. One might also mention in this connection the narrative tone or idiom which, in both narratives, is subject to very rapid fluctuations: bombast or pedantry will suddenly give way to sentiment, gentle wit and high-mindedness will be abruptly soured by fierce, crude black comedy. All these features give the narrative content its richness and density, but since their effects are not always compatible with one another the reader is naturally tempted to give more weight to one aspect and to consider the others in the light of it. Various manoeuvres and combinations are possible but the essential choice seems to be between approaches which focus primarily on the story and those which highlight the story-telling process. Let us now compare these features as potential keys to a reading of *Molloy*.[1]

Structure

What happens if we choose to emphasise the structural connection between the two narratives? Confronted by a maze of links, echoes, parallels, can we produce coherence? A prime obstacle is the fact that widely divergent orders of similarity are involved. For example:

1) Overall similarities between the two stories, which have the same circular structure, embody comparable obsessions with family relations, deploy comparable time-scales and spatial configurations (moving between landscape and interior) and reproduce broadly compatible scenarios of change, disintegration and ultimate failure.

2) 'Family resemblance' of particular scenes and episodes: both protagonists brutally assault a person in a forest; both

[1] For the sake of clarity, and space, I make no reference to specific critics in my discussion of approaches. The bibliography includes representative items for each of my categories; their critical orientation can usually be deduced from the title.

encounter a shepherd with his dog and flock; etc.

3) Correspondences of detail; similar 'properties' of the two narratives: the knife-rest, the wicker-gate, the red-lacquer tray, the straw boater, etc.

4) Verbal correspondences.

5) Equivalence of authorial situation: both protagonists give written accounts of their experiences; both are commissioned in some sense; both complain about the task.

What kind of narrative coherence can be coaxed or concocted out of this? Among the many problems one should perhaps single out a basic discrepancy: while some of the orders of similarity *do* tempt us to create a single, homogeneous narrative, others encourage us to regard the two narratives as *versions* of one another. In the former case we locate coherence (eventually) in the story; in the latter we locate it in the story-telling and see it as part of a design. Myth offers another level of reading that provides a way out of this dilemma, potentially allowing us to stay with the story.

Myth

At an initial level *Molloy* is 'mythic' by dint of dense, resonant images which seem to attest a powerful vision of man: Molloy, still far from his mother, propelling himself through the undergrowth using his crutches as grapnels; or Moran, his strange journey ended, smashing open the doors of his ruined residence. Taken as a whole, the novel seems to set up two poles: at one extreme, a recognisable social world (Molloy at the police-station, Moran at home); at the other a landscape pared down to essentials (sea, forest, plain). Molloy's brushes with officialdom, and Moran's relations with his household and neighbours, belong to recognisable fictional stereotypes, but their encounters with shepherds and charcoal-burners, and the rapid physical decline they both experience, enable the text to gain in symbolic power what it loses in verisimilitude. The sequences of events seem to conform to an underlying pattern — exile, fragmentation, homecoming, potential metamorphosis — which is mythic to the extent that it cannot easily be accounted for in social or psychological terms, while it echoes familiar archetypes. Myth can provide a strong incentive to cut through the tangles which seem to entwine the two narratives, and encourage us to reverse them. We then conceive of Moran in some sense 'turning into' Molloy, and the story is envisaged as a myth of initiation into a profounder, remoter, more authentic mode of being.

But as I have already suggested, this is not really consistent with the novel's overall structure. The narratives are in parallel as much as they are in series; the myth-hungry reader cannot readily appeal to the structure of the text for support. What then of the widespread mythic allusions in the text? Would these not confirm a mythic reading of the kind I have sketched? Both narratives contain explicit allusions to or obvious parallels with established myth: *The Odyssey* and quest narratives generally, the Old and New Testaments (especially the Passion), the modern myths of psychoanalysis. But, in their very multiplicity these allusions tend, I think, to dilute rather than to strengthen the overall mythic atmosphere. A highly selective approach which interprets the text in terms of a single set of mythic ingredients, Jungian or Christian for example, has to turn a blind eye to many aspects of the novel that will simply not fit.

Philosophy

In *Molloy*, philosophical ideas are, in their way, as pervasive as myths. Indeed one could argue that many of the episodes and encounters which seem wrapped in mythic density are, by a different token, the cruxes of philosophical debate concerning problems of identity, will and knowledge. Instead of being read in terms of myth the novel might be seen as a philosophical fable, drawing on aspects of the western philosophical tradition, and particularly Scholasticism, Cartesianism, British Empiricism, Scepticism. But the co-existence and intertwining of myth and philosophy in the text is detrimental to the scope of either. We may agree that Beckett translates some of Descartes's ideas into situations (Molloy's progress in the forest) or images (the bodily decline of the two protagonists), thereby, as one critic put

it, 'turning philosophy into myth' (*15*, p.41). But the mythic
power of, for example, the forest episode in Molloy's narrative
is diminished rather than enhanced if it is seen as the illustration
of a philosophical idea in which Beckett does not necessarily
believe; and the force of the philosophical idea is hardly
intensified by its assimilation to a mythic order only half-
heartedly endorsed by the text as a whole. Moreover, like the
myths, the philosophical ideas and references in *Molloy* are too
diffuse, piecemeal and unruly to provide a satisfactory key to
the text as a whole, even if they are sufficiently crucial and pervasive to require incorporation into any satisfactory account of
the text. By contrast with myth, philosophy features primarily in
the narrator's discourse where it tends to engender consternation
rather than certainty.

Narration

What, then, of narration? On what basis might it be considered the best starting-point for a reading of *Molloy*? We have
already noted the way the activity of narration is foregrounded
in the text, but clearly this would not necessarily give it pre-
eminence: narration, however prominent, could easily cor-
roborate and confirm another level of the text — its mythic or
philosophical or cryptic qualities. This is, however, far from
being the case, and it is the relative autonomy of the process of
narration in *Molloy* that must be taken into account. By autonomy I mean that the activity of narration is given its own
context in such a way that the story elements are seen to be
derivative of it. Far from being subservient to the story,
narration does not stand in a fixed, 'once and for all' relationship to it but shifts between various positions, setting up
different ratios of tale to telling. It is then, I think, the highly
inflected and problematic relationship between the process of
narration and what one may call the representation, or the story,
or the fiction, that takes us to the heart of *Molloy*. To explore
and substantiate this I want to turn now to the opening pages of
the novel.

BEGINNINGS

Molloy's account of his quest for his mother is preceded by two sequences: a passage (pp.7-8), separated from what follows by a paragraph break (the only one in his narrative) which serves as a kind of prologue; and, as a sort of 'prelude', the account (pp.8-19) of an incident that marked the beginning of the quest. Both texts are concerned with origins. Molloy says he is writing in his mother's room but he does not know how he got there. His narrative can therefore never bring us 'up to date'; there is an irreducible gap between the narration and its point of origin. He gives a highly implausible account of his motives for writing: a man collects the pages once a week in return for money. While Molloy denies that he writes for money, he is acutely aware of what 'they' want him to write, and to some extent complies with 'their' requirements. But while he would prefer to write about the present *they* seem to require that he write about his past.

What do we make of the narrative situation thus sketched in? It provides a motive for the text by explaining how and where it came to be written (and even, in theory, published). But it does so in a way that reminds us of the artifice on which all fictions depend. We are, it seems, given a gross parody of an archetypal authorial situation with its public and private dimensions. A man is writing in a room, drawing on the stuff of his own experience but complying with external criteria. In the course of Molloy's narrative proper we will frequently be made aware of the moment at which he writes but at no point will there be any further mention of his mother's room (without the prologue we shouldn't know that he ever got there) or of his 'employers'. The place of both is, it seems, taken by purely conventional features of discourse itself: the fact that it presupposes a writer and a reader. Each time the text reminds us of the process of writing itself we are potentially made aware of the empirical circumstances which this theoretically presupposes (though in a novel the only ones which underlie narration are those of the real author — here Samuel Beckett — and not the narrators). Equally, page after page, Molloy buttonholes the reader, constantly foregrounding the implied recipient, the 'vous' of literary communication, casting the reader in the role of his employers. The 'narratee' is deemed to incarnate rationality, to be cool, calm and collected; as such he is the butt of much ferocious irony as Molloy feigns but conspicuously fails to make his narrative conform with the norms he imputes to his readers.

When he gets round to introducing his narrative, Molloy emphasises that his 'employers' are unhappy about the way it begins. This is hardly surprising since in the sequence he refers to as his 'commencement' it takes him ten dense pages, full of equivocation and ambiguity, to reach the point at which he states, 'Je résolus d'aller voir ma mère' (p.19); and by the time he makes this announcement (expected since the novel's opening sentences) the reader, far from having been given an explanation of how Molloy came to be looking for his mother, has been exposed to a narrative idiom which makes it hard to talk in terms of events at all.

'Cette fois-ci, puis encore une je pense, puis c'en sera fini de ce monde-là aussi' (p.8): in the tones of a mumbled monologue, Molloy gives us the book's second beginning and a second frame of reference. His point of departure is no longer the relationship between his presence in a room and the world outside, but a symmetrical relationship between his mind ('c'est dans la tête') and its representations. He portrays himself as the passive and reluctant spectator of a sort of mental film — sounds and images which detain him in a world he thought he had relinquished — but in the very act of telling us this he makes an abrupt transition to a third and very different frame of reference.

Si l'on pense aux contours à la lumière de jadis c'est sans regret. Mais on n'y pense guère, avec quoi y penserait-on? Je ne sais pas. Il passe des gens aussi, dont il n'est pas facile de se distinguer avec netteté. Voilà qui est décourageant. C'est ainsi que je vis A et B aller lentement l'un vers l'autre. (p.9)

The long sequence about A and B is ostensibly introduced as an example of what happens when an event from Molloy's past comes into his mind. We probably expect the story to illustrate the lack of demarcation between what actually happened and subsequent subjective embroiderings. It does indeed do so but, without alerting us to the fact, Molloy narrates the episode primarily in terms of when it actually took place, thus ascribing the distortions and fantasies to the time of his encounter with A and B and not to the moment of recall.[2] Or rather he narrates the incident in such a way that the two contexts become totally fused with one another. The passage is one of Beckett's master-pieces and it repays close attention.

An empty road in open country a short way from town; every-thing is clear and distinct: 'une route ... sans haies ni murs, ni bordures d'aucune sorte ... balafrait les tendres pâturages' (p.9). Above the road, in the lee of a large outcrop of rock, a shadowy, indistinct figure: 'J'étais juché au-dessus du niveau le plus élevé de la route et plaqué par-dessus le marché contre un rocher de la même couleur que moi, je veux dire gris' (p.12). At a relatively short interval, two men walk out from the direction of the town along the road beneath the rock; one returns, appears to exchange a few words with the other, then both continue on their way, one back towards the town, the other into the hills. In no time this anecdotal skeleton is fleshed out by conjectures: the grey speck transforms the landscape; Molloy's speculations rapidly undermine the empirical distinctiveness of A, B and himself. The two men, arbitrarily and schematically designated, become poles in a series of thematic and mythic tensions between town and country, near and far, society and solitude, personality and anonymity. Around B Molloy weaves a beauti-ful fantasy of weariness, renunciation, and departure. The man is setting off into the hills he has previously only glimpsed from afar; perhaps he will never return. The arbitrariness of this scenario is at times fully acknowledged: 'Je le regardai s'éloigner, gagné par son inquiétude, enfin par une inquiétude qui n'était pas nécessairement la sienne, mais dont il faisait en quelque sorte partie. C'était, qui sait, mon inquiétude à moi qui le gagnait lui' (p.12). Still, the figure of B seems to lend itself to the fantasy. In the case of A, however, Molloy seems wilfully to

[2] 'The observer infects the observed with his own mobility', as Beckett wrote of Proust's narrator (5, p.17).

introduce indeterminacy. Everything about the man suggests that he is a city-dweller out for an evening stroll, but Molloy picks at details, casts doubt on his faculties of observation and invents ambiguities which could allow for the possibility that A, too, is in the grip of despair and social alienation: 'il en était peut-être là, malgré les apparences' (p.14).

So far what has been to the fore is the space between perceiver and world, between Molloy and A and B. And we can identify three strands in this relationship. First it implies a set of philosophical questions concerning mind and world, subjectivity and objectivity, thought and perception. Then, filling these out with specific human content, we can detect a range of affective factors: desire, fears, the tendency to identification which seems to structure Molloy's engagement with what he sees. Thirdly we can see that the effect of these factors is, through distortion, to mythologise what is perceived. Already the mythic territory and the philosophical dimension that will characterise Molloy's narrative are established. But we have not yet considered the narrative framework which gives us access to the relationship between Molloy and the world, a central feature of which is the distance it creates between the narrator and the figure crouched by his rock. How is this effect of distance achieved, what is its nature and what effect does it have? The first thing we must do is identify, within the narrative framework, a second context in which the terms are not consciousness and world but consciousness and narration. Let us look at the passage where, having imagined what might have ensued had he accosted A, inspected the man's dog, cigar, shoes (all clues to his status) at close range, and asked him where he was going, Molloy observes that in not doing so he retained a peculiar kind of freedom:

> Et je suis à nouveau je ne dirai pas seul ... libre ... libre de quoi faire, de ne rien faire, de savoir, mais quoi, les lois de la conscience peut-être, de ma conscience, que par exemple l'eau monte à mesure qu'on s'y enfonce et qu'on ferait mieux, enfin aussi bien, d'effacer les textes que de noircir les marges, de les boucher jusqu'à ce que tout soit blanc et lisse et que la connerie prenne son vrai visage, un

non-sens cul et sans issue. Je fis donc bien sans doute,
enfin aussi bien, de ne pas me déranger de mon poste
d'observation. Mais au lieu d'observer j'eus la faiblesse de
retourner en esprit vers l'autre, vers l'homme au bâton. Ce
fut alors à nouveau les murmures. (pp.15-16)

With the aid of the present tense, two time-scales are fused
here. In the context of the action or representation Molloy,
having decided not to accost A, is free to dwell on the fact that
since the more information the mind is given the more hypotheses it will invent ('l'eau monte à mesure qu'on s'y enfonce')
he was better off not finding out more about A. While in the
second context, of narration or writing, it is suggested that the
less said about A (or anything else) the better, since it would be
best to refrain from narration altogether. Here the two contexts
match: Molloy's 'faiblesse' which leads his thoughts back to B
corresponds to the narrator's 'faiblesse' in continuing to record
Molloy's thoughts and hence not following his own precept.
However, a few pages further on we are told, again in the
present tense:

Je confonds peut-être plusieurs occasions différentes ... Et
ce fut peut-être un jour A à tel endroit, puis un autre B à tel
autre, puis un troisième le rocher et moi, et ainsi de suite
pour les autres composants, les vaches, le ciel, la mer, les
montagnes. (p.17)

Obviously here, only the context and moment of narration are
relevant and what is at issue is not simply the degree of
distortion to which consciousness or memory submit events and
perceptions but the prior existence of any experience corres-
ponding to what has been narrated.

The A and B sequence culminates in a passage which links it to
the quest narrative that is to follow. Molloy wonders if he is
right in thinking that he never saw A and B again, and then asks:

Et qu'est-ce que j'appelle voir et revoir? ... De la fumée,
des bâtons, de la chair, des cheveux, le soir, autour du

désir d'un frère. Ces haillons je sais les susciter, pour en couvrir ma honte. Je me demande ce que ça veut dire. Mais je ne serai pas toujours dans le besoin. Mais à propos du désir d'un frère je dirai que m'étant réveillé entre onze heures et midi (j'entendis l'angélus, rappelant l'incarnation, peu de temps après) je résolus d'aller voir ma mère. (p.18)

Once again the two contexts — narration and representation — interpenetrate and the burden of the passage can be interpreted in terms of either. In the context of representation the process we have already recognised is made explicit: perception, for Molloy, consists in an activity of *fabrication*. Affective pressures translate what is seen into scenarios reflecting underlying needs. The strong element of identification and desire for human contact perceptible throughout the episode is also acknowledged in the phrase 'désir d'un frère' and its link to the resolution to go in quest of his mother. But certain features of the passage which remain very enigmatic in this framework make more sense when read in the context of narration: the verb *susciter* which suggests a mental activity working on representations rather than on things directly perceived; the extreme fragmentation of the ingredients echoing the earlier passage; the emphasis on deficiency and lack: 'désir d'un frère', 'couvrir me honte', 'le besoin'. All these make the passage coherent as an evocation of the process of narration conceived as a transformation and reorganisation of past perceptions and experiences, actual or hypothetical, personal or impersonal. The process aims, it appears, to fulfil a need and to fill a gap, but this has less to do with a need for others than with a desire to give some sort of substance to one's sense of self: 'Ces haillons, je sais les susciter pour en couvrir ma honte'. It is as if the narrator were giving away the tricks of his trade: to construct A and B — and Molloy's quest by his rock for that matter — out of scraps lying around in one's memory is to disguise the shame that accompanies direct self-confrontation.[3] All the 'events' and

---

[3] This phrase reminds me of the opening of Mallarmé's 'L'Après-midi d'un faune': the faun proclaims, 'Ces nymphes, je les veux perpétuer', and then

'adventures' presented ('suscités') in the text are perhaps to be conceived as disguises, and Molloy's quest for his mother should perhaps be seen as no more nor less than a disguise to hide the narrator's shame, a fiction generated by anxiety, with only a tenuous link to any experience prior to it.

In this extraordinary and brilliant piece of prose three contexts — someone making up a story, someone recalling past events, someone deciphering what he observes — are woven together in a single process of narration which converts them into symptoms of divergent anxieties, needs and desires. Some of these find their expression in the construction of a story, in the enactment of an image of an individual's past and of existence in a recognisable world, while others seek to repudiate or dissolve such a picture, to denounce it as a fiction and to refuse it credence. Conflicting images of the self seem bound up with this and especially these two: an image of the self as a coherent entity, rooted in experience in the world, finding its definition in such categories as action and event; and, conversely, an image of the self as something shapeless, undefined, inner rather than outer, timeless rather than timebound. But the conflict played out in the narration is not simply an oscillation between two competing images. The former — that of a self more or less integrated with a world outside it — is never really considered viable, and is always associated with the realm of fiction and make-believe; it is a fantasy the narrator cherishes, and he entertains it not because he believes in it but because if he could believe it he would earn some respite from the burden of confronting the other, literally unthinkable, alternative. This is, I think, what is explicitly formulated by two of the inter-polations, the discursive asides, which occur in the course of Molloy's account of an imaginary conversation with A (it is explicitly stated not to have taken place). The first: 'Ce dont j'ai besoin c'est des histoires j'ai mis longtemps à le savoir' (p.15), conveys the pleasure of an excursion into an explicitly hypo-thetical, and hence fictional dimension. The second: 'Dire que je fais de mon mieux pour ne pas parler de moi' (ibid.), is doubly

proceeds to construct an erotic fantasy round his brief glimpse of young maidens bathing.

revealing in that it suggests both that the motive for inventing stories is the desire not to speak about oneself, and the awareness that whatever one writes, however fictional, is self-revealing.

If one dominant tack in the narration is to lose oneself in stories, the other is in some ways simply a recognition of the impossiblity of doing so; it is the assertion that this 'won't do', that one 'can't keep it up', that one is something quite other than 'a story', though quite what remains to be seen. In *Molloy*, then, an ontological conflict is played out in and through a process of narration.

To conclude this discussion of the opening of the novel, I should like to link it to what I said about approaches. The first observation we can make is that it is the urge to produce fictions that engenders the mythic dimension of the text. Indeed the essence of this sequence is the demonstration that the whole realm of representation in the text, the story, the characters (including Molloy), the settings, the plot, are all reflections of an underlying narrative situation. The often contradictory features which characterise these ingredients reflect contradictions and pressures within this narrative situation. One set of factors lends reality and credibility to Molloy's adventures, another attempts to deprive them of these; one set lends mythic and philosophical overtones, another discredits them; one set treats events as if they had happened, another urges us to construe them as arbitrary building blocks to construct fictions. In a single 'story', the same elements are being pulled in different directions. Everything represented in the text bears signs of its plural origin, its divided affiliations and air of intermediacy. And the figure of Molloy seems to originate in and exemplify perfectly this very intermediacy, not least by what it borrows from the stereotype of the tramp, that misfit *par excellence*, to whom I shall return.

I suggested earlier that in approaching *Molloy* we were confronted with a choice between story and story-telling process. In arguing why I have chosen the latter, I hope to have stressed adequately that such a choice does not dispose once and for all of myth and philosophy and cryptic clues. Far from it. In the remainder of this book I shall be seeking to demonstrate the ways in which the narrative process of *Molloy* produces these dimensions of the text, and to identify the essential function they retain in our sense of its range of meaning. In this connection it will be useful to consider at this point some aspects of the context in which Beckett wrote *Molloy*.

BECKETT, FICTION, FORM

Molloy was written in 1947-48, when Beckett was in the midst of an extraordinary burst of creativity to which we owe not only this novel and the further two it spawned, but also four long short-stories and two plays: the unpublished *Eleutheria*, and *En attendant Godot* which was to bring the author world-wide fame as a dramatist. This period begins with Beckett's return to his Paris flat after the war in 1946. For two years, so legend has it, he scarcely left his room and wrote day and night. Thereafter there were brief spells when other, usually material, consider-ations preoccupied him, but in 1948-49 he once again retired to his room and wrote *Malone meurt*, a first outgrowth of *Molloy*, and then *L'Innommable*.[4] The resulting trilogy of novels is the heartland of Beckett's work and it would be no exaggeration to say that all his subsequent writing in whatever medium draws on it constantly.[5] Moreover to recognise this is also to acknowledge the particular centrality of *Molloy* in Beckett's work: gathering together a number of crucial strands in his earlier writings, but also twisting them to a new pattern, it marked a decisive culmination; initiating and feeding other novels and texts it constituted a new beginning. Like many a masterpiece *Molloy* both consolidates and inaugurates.

Perhaps the single most decisive feature distinguishing *Molloy* from the two novels (*Murphy*, 1938; *Watt*, 1945) Beckett had already published is his adoption of a form of first-person narration closely allied to monologue (the other major

---

[4] For details of this period see the chapter in Bair entitled '1946-48: The Siege in the Room', *28*, pp.346-80.

[5] For brief discussion of the other two novels see the last section of chapter 4 below.

innovations — writing in French, the paring down of detail and external reference-points, the two-part structure — can be seen as major symptoms within the same syndrome).[6] Monologue was of course by this time a staple ingredient of modern fictional writing[7]. It had been adopted primarily by novelists who wished to render, in Bergson's phrase, 'les données immédiates de la conscience' and to allow the reader 'direct' access to the character's mind by cutting out the mediation of a narrator. Characteristically this procedure implied a commitment to a vision of the self which pitted individual consciousness against the hostilities of the social world, and monologue tended to represent the authentic as against the adventitious dimension of the personality. Beckett's use of monologue in the 'Nouvelles' — the four long short-stories of 1945-46 in which he first used the form — departs, though still somewhat tentatively, from many of the basic assumptions underlying the use of this device in modern fiction; in *Molloy* the break is radical. The modernist tradition in fiction had tended to make individual self-consciousness the site of manifold representations of the world, integrated, if often *in extremis*, by a key reference point — the singular individual and his subjectivity. It is the status of this reference-point that Beckett's work from *Molloy* onwards, explores and puts into question. Monologue is employed within a fictional structure which emphasises division. The fictive situation is designed in such a way that there is no current input of experience (the narrator is characteristically sealed away in a room, like Beckett ...) and this tends to foreground tension between the monologist's consciousness and its existing accumulation of mental 'material'. But at the same time, the 'present' context is given the character of an imposed task, which is held to account for its written form (written monologue

[6] *Molloy* was the first major work Beckett wrote in French. I associate his writing in a 'second language' with other symptoms of his desire to create effects of strangeness and distance, especially where narrative voice is concerned. The decision to write plays (in the same period) was another symptomatic move. The two-part structure, employed in the two acts of *Godot* (and the original plan of *Fin de partie*) creates distance by denying the authority of any single 'version' of a story.

[7] For excellent discussions of monologue and related modes of narration see Cohn, *35, passim*.

is of course already an uneasy notion). Moreover the incorporation of the act of writing (as opposed to merely 'thinking'),
together with the orientation towards the past, links the device
to first-person autobiographical narratives — *David Copper-
field* would be a typical example — which tend to involve a
dissonance between the mature self who writes and the youthful
self who is the protagonist. Combining elements from various
fictional modes, Beckett creates a narrative structure which in its
articulation of the relationship between narrator, world, time,
experience, and medium, offers maximum scope for division
and irresolution in the area of the self. It would be a large and
hazardous task to attempt to explain how Beckett arrived at the
fictional form which is so characteristic of the work that the
Beckett narrative voice is instantly recognisable, but some of the
more significant stages may usefully be indicated.

One of Beckett's earliest publications was a critical essay (*4*)
on Joyce's *Work in Progress* (eventually *Finnegans Wake*); this
was followed, a few months later, by his first book: a brief and
trenchant study (*5*) of Proust's *A la recherche du temps perdu*.
Meditation on the great innovatory novelists of the age marked a
crucial phase in Beckett's evolution as a writer. In our present
perspective what is significant about *Proust* (1931) is the
constant emphasis on 'Proust's pessimism'. In Beckett's eyes
Proust is not so much the celebrant of time regained as of time
'obliterated'. The famous moments of illumination in *A la
recherche* are not read as intimations of the aesthetic vocation
which will eventually lead to the recapture and transfiguration
of the past, but as 'mystical experiences' which lead the narrator
towards a total denial of time and experience. By the same token
Beckett's Proust is the great novelist of separation: the self is
unknowable, so are other people, love is impossible, friendship
no better, we are trapped in our minds, and so forth. To escape
all this is to escape *into* another order which reveals all the more
clearly, as lightning illuminates a landscape, the nullity of everything else. Beckett draws frequent attention to devices which
underline and implement separation, for example 'Proust's
impressionism' which goes beyond relativism and consists in the
'non-logical statement of phenomena in the order and exactitude

of their perception, before they have been distorted into intelligibility in order to be forced into a chain of cause and effect' (*5*, p.86) — as a fictional device this will occur frequently in *Molloy*. He also argues that Proust, like Dostoevsky 'states his characters without explaining them', or rather 'Proust's explanations are experimental and not demonstrative. He explains them in order that they may appear as they are — inexplicable. He explains them away' (*5*, p.87). This is both a perceptive comment on Proust and an indication of the kind of status explanation will have in Beckett's own work.

The essay on Joyce is devoted primarily to the role of philosophical ideas in *Work in Progress*. Beckett is at pains to warn potential readers against the pitfalls of assuming that Joyce subscribes to or endorses the ideas he uses: 'Vico's social and historical classification', we are told, 'is clearly adapted by Mr Joyce as a structural convenience — or inconvenience' (*4*, p.7); this is well worth bearing in mind when considering the role of philosophical allusions in *Molloy*. To make the point another way Beckett insists on the indivisibility of form and content in Joyce's work: 'Here form *is* content, content *is* form ... his writing is not about something it is that something itself' (*4*, p.13). But Beckett is clearly uneasy about the way stress placed on aesthetic form can itself serve a specific vision of reality, one which sees in form the realisation of an underlying harmony and coherence. To counter this he emphasises in Joyce's case mitigating factors. For example, with aesthetic pattern in mind, we are told that while 'Dante's [purgatory] is conical and consequently implies culmination, Mr Joyce's is spherical and excludes culmination' (*4*, p.21); and as for Joyce's style, its 'inner elemental vitality and corruption of expression imparts a furious restlessness to the form' so that 'a continuous purgatorial process is at work'. If in Joyce and Proust, artistic vision aspires to paradise, artistic process keeps us in purgatory — or tries to. When he subsequently recognised the extent to which Joyce was, as he put it, an 'Apollonian' artist, 'tending towards omniscience and omnipotence', Beckett distinguished himself from his erstwhile mentor in the strongest of terms.[8]

[8] 'The more Joyce knew the more he could. He's tending towards omniscience

At the heart of Beckett's reading of Proust and Joyce are two oppositions: between inner and outer worlds, and between aesthetic form and the chaos of experience; and he is particularly sensitive to the temptations — omnipresent and finally victorious in the writers he studied — of squashing these distinctions into one so that the inner world becomes the witness and guarantor of a unity beneath the world's chaos. In the high modernist tradition to which Proust and Joyce belong (with Woolf, Mann, Faulkner, Musil) the figure of the artist often plays a crucial role in this respect. The artistic sensibility is made to represent a form of consciousness which, in its very solitude and rarity, holds the key to a vision of the world as a totality. Beckett's work is deeply imbued with this tradition, and he is fascinated by the temptation to which Joyce and Proust succumbed. Nevertheless he repudiates it; and in doing so he seeks to keep open the breaches they mended. Aesthetic form will, in his work, frequently be *contrasted* ironically with experience, and individual consciousness will constantly remain distanced from the world. This latter division — between inner and outer worlds — permeates Beckett's first published novel. At the core of *Murphy* is the utterly dualistic picture of consciousness Beckett identified (and relished) in Proust: Murphy is a 'seedy solipsist' who spends his happiest hours in a rocking-chair, obliterating the outer world and attempting to 'come alive in his mind'. A whole chapter is devoted to Murphy's mind, or rather to his conception of it: 'what he called his mind functioned not as an instrument but as a place'. The image of mind as place will subsequently haunt all Beckett's work, although in a crucially different manner: whereas Murphy's is described from the outside, the mind in *Molloy* and subsequent novels becomes the locale in which the activity of narration originates. The difference is crucial. For all its adumbration of Beckettian motifs *Murphy* remains within the tradition of comic novels of character. The eccentric protagonist

and omnipotence as an artist. I'm working with impotence, ignorance ... I think anyone nowadays who pays the slightest attention to his experience finds it the experience of a non-knower, or a non-canner. The other type of artist — the Apollonian — is absolutely foreign to me.' Israel Shenker, 'An Interview with Beckett', *New York Times*, 5th May 1956 (collected in *29*, p.148).

is presented to us by a third-person narrative voice which, for all its vigour and verbal luxuriance, is essentially anonymous and inert; it shows us, on one side, Murphy and his mind and, on the other, a motley crew of amusing stereotypes — Irish *literati*, London landladies, people loose in their morals and loose in the head. The latter represent the social world and the action sets them in pursuit of Murphy who, in his flight from the various demands and definitions others wish to foist on him, tries a succession of refuges before eventually meeting his death by a preposterous accident in a mental hospital.

We are now in a better position to appreciate what, in the context of a darker and deeper modulation of his vision, monologue represented to Beckett when he adopted it, at first tentatively in the *nouvelles*, and then triumphantly in *Molloy*. Essential here is this paradox: while it appears to do away with the division between narrative voice and central character, by fusing them in the figure of the monologist, in Beckett's hands the device in fact maintains the division in another more fruitful and significant form, as a manifestation of the split between mind (the activities of consciousness), and body (existence in space, time, the world of others). Instead of simply uniting narrative voice and protagonist, monologue makes them at once identical and alien to one another. The construction of the narrative situation is crucial here. In Beckett the monologist's discourse is always severed from immediate contact with the world and addresses itself to the past or the future, or to a process of hypothesis or invention. This means that we are always aware of two contexts: the person in the room, speaking, writing, thinking; and the representations of a remembered, or imagined, or invented self, out there in the world. In the logic of Beckett's development as a writer the shift to monologue is not a move inside, *into* the solipsistic world but towards a fictional form which produces a sense of the divided nature of consciousness, and which, in an essentially exploratory and tentative mode, enacts the processes through which a disenfranchised self both seeks and evades representation.

2. Incarnations: Molloy

At the origin of Molloy's quest is the image of incarnation: 'm'étant réveillé entre onze heures et midi (j'entendis l'angélus, rappelant l'incarnation, peu de temps après) je résolus d'aller voir ma mère' (p.19). The mind raking over its embers, the man writing in his room, project themselves, by an act of creation, into the outer world and find (or seek) incarnation. At the heart of the idea of incarnation is the mysterious conjunction of two worlds or planes customarily separate: sacred and profane, eternal and temporal. The divine, for example, takes on the trappings of the human: flesh and blood, place and time. Part of the mystery of incarnation is that the integration of the two realms is only partial, the one subsists in the other, sometimes obtrusively. What, then, makes the *tramp* so fitting an incarnation for the man in the room?

The tramp is inherently marginal, belonging neither to country nor town; provisional in his living arrangements, of no fixed abode or purpose, constantly forced to adjust to new circumstances but remaining within the bounds of a strictly limited range of possibilities, repeated in random order, he is constantly in transit. His relations with society are intermittent and often fretful; he is shy of authority, ill-adapted to ordinary social intercourse, and he dreads above all having to *account* for himself. His few possessions are of uncertain provenance and easily take on a fetishistic or talismanic status. He views the world from an angle at which activities other humans take for granted seem strange; severed from utilitarian considerations, but spasmodically purposeful in the pursuit of short-term objectives, the tramp's itinerary tends to blur the distinctions between places, reducing them to their archetype: town, sea and marsh, forest. The 'gentleman of the road' frequently exhibits traces of ruined gentility: morsels of knowledge, cultural reference, and an immemorial past punctuate his ruminations.

He is afflicted by minor ailments, yet bodily dilapidation never seems to threaten his longevity.

The tramp is the embodiment of Beckett's world. He epitomises emblematically all the dissociations which provide Molloy's narrative with its dominant thematic and structural features. Three main areas of disjunction can be distinguished. Firstly, disparity between outer appearance and inner disposition. Secondly, disparities between the instruments of knowledge — analytical thought, calculation, logic, culture — and empirical experience. Thirdly, disparity between the present in which we write and reflect and the past in which we existed. Each finds its incarnation in the tramp's features: his autistic shyness, the difficulty he has in complying with social norms, his lack of autobiographical bearings. These three areas will provide us with keys for our analysis.

Molloy's narrative of the quest for his mother falls naturally into three roughly equal parts. The first comprises his journey from the countryside into the town where his mother may reside, his encounters with officialdom which drive him back to the country, and his subsequent return to the town. The second concerns his stay at the house of a woman he calls Lousse. In the third part Molloy heads for the country again, spends a period by the sea, then makes his way (with increasing difficulty due to his physical deterioration) through the forest to a point from where he can glimpse the town. Here his narrative ends. In this chapter I shall examine these three parts in turn.

TOWN AND COUNTRY

(a) Complementary forms of self-dissociation mark Molloy's experiences in town and countryside. The town, with its bureaucracy, citizenry and constabulary is a microcosm of institutionalised society predicated on firm social roles: policeman, official, charity-worker, tramp. The surrounding rural area, given over to small-scale agriculture and farming, is equally rigid and static. In creating so vivid a picture with so few means, Beckett draws to great effect on his experience of Ireland in the first quarter of the century. By comparison with, say,

Watt, the specifically Irish elements are few; moreover, writing in French, and the mixing of Irish and French proper names, tends to neutralise the setting; yet no-one would, I think, fail to register the Irish atmosphere. The result is a strange amalgam of the highly local, specific and realistic with the wholly artificial and alien.

Molloy's alienation in both settings does not serve to define his essence so much as to stress his lack of essence. In the town self-dissociation stems from his awareness of the gap that separates him from the image other people have of him. As the object of the policeman's censure (p.25), the official's inquisitiveness (p.28), the social-worker's charity (p.30), Molloy is invited to comply with stereotypes based on presuppositions (for example, that he knows the regulations concerning bicycles, that he ought to know his name, that he will be grateful for a free bite) which are perfectly logical but which simply do not happen to apply to him. And because these suppositions do not apply, the sense of identity they could offer is unavailable to Molloy. To talk in these terms is of course to do scant justice to the fierce, satirical comedy of those scenes which contrast social definitions of selfhood with the specificity of an individual life. But it would be to miss the point if we assumed that in registering the inner distance which separates him from the cate-gorised self defined by the policeman and his cohorts, Molloy could readily refer to an alternative, more authentic self-image available in his own consciousness rather than mirrored in theirs. If there is something comforting about the belief that we are more truly ourselves in our inner life than in our social personae, it is as well to bear in mind that Molloy has few illusions on this score. Noting that as the policeman firmly guides him through the streets he can contentedly dissociate himself from the scene: 'Je me donnais à cet instant doré, comme si j'avais été un autre' (p.26), Molloy goes on to observe: 'Je tirais vers ce faux profond, aux fausses allures de gravité et de paix, je m'y élançais de tous mes vieux poisons' (p.26), emphatically recognising that the inner life is as much the realm of illusion as the outer, while acknowledging (in a way that anticipates Moran) the intoxicating allure of apparently profounder images of selfhood.

Molloy's flights to the countryside seem to correspond to a desire to escape definition and to lose consciousness of self. Lying in a ditch, eating grass, obscured by drizzle, apparently invisible to a passing canal boatman and a shepherd (who ignores the question he asks him), Molloy seems about to achieve a sort of osmosis with the environment. But his eclipse is never more than partial: even if his body seems to achieve a sort of quiescence, consciousness reasserts itself in the form of anxiety and irresolution, suddenly reiterating the impulse to seek his mother (p.38) or rekindling doubts about the destination of the sheep (this had been the subject of Molloy's question to the shepherd). Molloy fails, then, to coincide with either an 'urban' form of selfhood, based on the existence of others, or a 'pastoral' one associated with archaic, archetypal forms of consciousness.

(b) Some of the disjunctions which figure prominently in the discursive passages rather than in the fictive situations themselves, can be associated with the two settings, urban and rural. In the town Molloy, having been, to his surprise, released from custody, reflects that had he been better educated he would have conformed more naturally to the social codes he has transgressed and which have landed him in trouble. This leads to a very funny excursus (p.32) where the comedy springs from the supposition that civilised behaviour is an arcane system the first principles of which must be thoroughly mastered before their application to specific human activities can be attempted. The underlying opposition between the contingent realm of empirical experience and the abstract realm of principles will be repeated in numerous forms throughout *Molloy*. Closely linked with it is the opposition between the senses and the intelligence. Instead of being synchronised, perception and ratiocination tend for Molloy to alternate. A thing will engage his attention as a pure phenomenon, a meaningless cluster of shapes and qualities. For instance the cup, saucer and bread provided by the charity-worker is described as a 'petit amas d'objets hétérogènes et branlants, où voisinaient le dur, le liquide et le mou' (p.30). By

the time Molloy's perceptions begin to settle into intelligible
patterns, either the thing has vanished or his conjectures create
ambiguities that further enquiries tend to exacerbate rather than
dispel. While he tends, comically, to blame the state of his
senses, it is evident that his lack of social integration makes him
pursue any issue — such as the destination of the sheep (p.38) —
as if it were a problem of pure knowledge rather than contingent, context-bound fact; and there is an evident connection
between his sense of inner anonymity, the indeterminacy of the
world as he perceives it, and the sense of a gulf between words
and things: 'la sensation de ma personne s'enveloppait d'un
anonymat souvent difficile à percer ... Et ainsi de suite pour les
autres objets qui me bafouaient les sens ... la condition de
l'objet était d'être sans nom, et inversement' (p.40).

Molloy's impulse to find his mother involves a further sort of
disparity. An overall disjunction between impulse and execution
embraces a set of related dichotomies: mind and will, will and
action, action and result. The impulse is always sudden (pp.19,
35, 38) and seems to come from outside his immediate concerns.
To translate it into action he needs to fill it out with reasons and
justifications, but these have no necessary relation to the
impulse itself, and since they pitch him into the contingent world
of actions and events, they tend to be subject to rapid erosion:
'Debout dans le fossé j'appelai à mon secours les bonnes raisons
que j'avais pour y aller ... Mes pieds, voyez-vous, ne me
conduisaient jamais chez ma mère sans une injonction de plus
haut, à cet effet' (p.38). The elaborate vignette, with its geriatric
gallows-humour (pp.20-24), depicting Molloy's earlier visits to
his mother delays the narrative with an image of his goal that
serves as a perpetual foil to the mock-epic earnestness of the
quest. The fact that this is the only content Molloy can give to
the experience of visiting his mother does not diminish the
impulse but it does tend to deny it any evident motive. Not
surprisingly, Molloy is inclined to forget the reasons he invents,
but this links up with wider oppositions:

Mes raisons? Je les avais oubliées. Mais je les connaissais,
je croyais les connaître, je n'avais qu'à les retrouver pour

que j'y vole, chez ma mère, sur les ailes de poules de la nécessité. Oui, du moment qu'on sait pourquoi tout devient facile, une simple question de magie. Connaître le saint, tout est là, n'importe quel con peut s'y vouer. Pour les détails, ... il n'y a pas à se désespérer ... C'est pour l'ensemble qu'il ne semble pas exister de grimoire. Peut-être qu'il n'y a pas d'ensemble, sinon posthume. (p.35)

'La nécessité', 'magie', 'le saint', 'l'ensemble', 'le grimoire', are all terms designating potential harmony between empirical circumstance and inner impulse, between experience and coherence. The speculation that such a resolution is possible only posthumously may seem to be little else than a quip. But the narrating Molloy regards his current immobility (his last steps, he informs us, were 'éxécutés l'année dernière', p.32) as a definitive retreat akin to death and feels that he ought to benefit from a posthumous perspective; he complains however that it is 'inutile de se savoir défunt, on ne l'est pas, on se tortille encore ... on se rend à l'évidence, ce n'est pas soi qui est mort c'est tous les autres. Alors on se lève et on va chez sa mère qui se croit vivante' (p.35). This curious passage makes it clear that the contradictions displayed in Molloy's experiences duplicate those he feels currently as he narrates: 'going to see one's mother' becomes a kind of shorthand for resolving once and for all the loose ends which persist even when experience is to all intents and purposes over. But the very fact that one still exists to think about it creates a loose end and makes the project an interminable one.

If Molloy's quest for his mother — 'cet irréel voyage, pénultième d'une forme pâlissante entre formes pâlissantes' (p.20) — consists in no more nor less than its narration, the dialectic between the idiom of lived experience and that of imaginative fabrication is itself fundamental to the narrator's sense of his circumstances: 'Ma vie, ma vie, tantôt j'en parle comme d'une chose finie, tantôt comme d'une plaisanterie qui dure encore, et j'ai tort, car elle est finie et elle dure à la fois, mais par quel temps du verbe exprimer cela?' (p.47).

(c) In fact the most intrusive narratorial interventions in the first third of Molloy's narrative not only reiterate the opposition between life and death but interrupt and question the passages which formulate discursively the oppositions that Molloy's experience seems to manifest. One instance among many is this coda to the passage where Molloy had neatly formulated his sense of the irreducible heterogeneity of words and things:

> Je dis ça maintenant, mais au fond qu'en sais-je maintenant, de cette époque, maintenant que grêlent sur moi les mots glacés de sens et que le monde meurt aussi, lâchement, lourdement nommé? J'en sais ce que savent les mots et les choses mortes et ça fait une jolie petite somme, un commencement, un milieu et une fin, comme dans les phrases bien bâties et dans la longue sonate des cadavres.
> (p.41)

Again the claims of the present to confer intelligibility on the past are repudiated. Retrospective verbal formulation, deploying words heavy and dense with meaning in the set patterns of prose, is now associated with death. Words usurp the experiences they are supposed to serve. The recurrent narration of Molloy's experiences comes to be identified with the narrator's sense of his inability to express himself in ways which do anything but repeat, in falsely organised form, the contradictions inherent in his current experience. Seeking to exorcise his past, he succeeds only in allowing it to proliferate in the jungle of words and fictions. If Molloy is constantly jerked from immobility into activity, it is because the narrator feels constrained to keep on narrating. And just as Molloy needs to find reasons to fill out the impulse to see his mother so the narrator keeps finding, and then repudiating, motives to fill out the sheer impulse to go on:

> Mais il va falloir que je me sorte de ce fossé ... J'y reviendrai sans doute un jour, ou dans une dépression analogue, je fais confiance à mes pieds pour cela ... Et si,

trop changé pour les reconnaître, je ne précise pas que ce
sont les mêmes, ne vous y trompez pas, ce seront les
mêmes, quoique changés. Car camper un être, un endroit,
j'allais dire une heure, mais je ne veux offenser personne,
et ensuite ne plus s'en servir, ce serait, comment dire, je ne
sais pas. Ne pas vouloir dire, ne pas savoir ce qu'on veut
dire, ne pas pouvoir ce qu'on croit qu'on veut dire, et
toujours dire ou presque, voilà ce qu'il importe de ne pas
perdre de vue, dans la chaleur de la rédaction. (pp.35-36)

Both the fact that in the 'story', Molloy does get up from his
ditch and the fact that he will indeed end up in another one, at
the end of his narrative (p.122) are seen to be determined by the
fact that as long as the narrator keeps narrating Molloy will keep
moving, condemned to a small circle of situations the apparent
distinctiveness of which is illusory. If we now turn to the second
sequence of Molloy's narrative — his stay at Mme Lousse's
house — we must seek to explain both the transformations that
Molloy's experiences undergo and their underlying conformity
to patterns already established in the text.

CHEZ MME LOUSSE

Molloy's stay at the house of the woman he refers to as Lousse
is like the central panel of a triptych — an interior flanked by
two exteriors. In terms of the text's faint but persistent Christian
imagery it constitutes the death and burial which followed the
incarnation and precedes Molloy's resurrection in his own
region in the last third of the book. Having run over Teddy,
Lousse's dog, Molloy is unable to help her bury him but reflects,
'j'y contribuais de ma présence. Comme si ç'avait été mon
enterrement à moi. Et il l'était' (p.48). Towards the end the
narrator three times denies this period any particular significance (pp.68, 71, 74), noting at one point: 'Cette période de ma
vie. Elle me fait penser, quand j'y pense, à de l'air dans une
conduite d'eau' (p.71). This seems a reflection not only of
Molloy's temporary extrication from the realm of purpose and
action, but of a pause in the narrator's concern with the

plausibility of Molloy's actions. For the narrator's hand is now more evident and the artifice more flagrant than before.

In this section the interaction of narration and representation can be characterised in terms of a notion of travesty. The circumstances in which Molloy is taken in as a substitute pet by an eccentric old lady living alone in a large house with a yellow-waistcoated manservant, a bilingual parrot and a great many antiques, are themselves handled in a way that makes them a travesty (i.e. a deliberately gross parody) of what such a situation would be 'in real life' or in another sort of book. Moreover, at a narrative level, this sequence also travesties the archetypal situation and images to which it subtly alludes: the Renaissance *topos* of the 'bower of bliss', Ulysses's enchantment by Circe, etc. But in a more fundamental way Molloy's adventures at Mme Lousse's house are a travesty of the narrator's own preoccupations as he writes and cogitates in his room (while these are, in turn, a travesty of Samuel Beckett writing in his room...). Similarly Molloy, within the representation, tries to find logical explanations for problems such as why his room keeps changing, why he stayed at Lousse's house as long as he did, why time seems to have gone haywire, which are as they are not for any logical or necessary reason, but simply because the story requires it or stipulates it; these problems originate, in other words, outside the realm of the representation, in that of the narration. Polarised in this way, narration and representation come to stand for divergent, but simultaneous, dimensions of experience, mental and physical, and as such serve to present a powerful image of human reality. To exist in both a mind — the realm of memory, desire, anticipation, imagination, anxiety — and a body — tied to space and time — is, we are invited to surmise, to be a walking travesty like hairy old Molloy dolled up in Mrs Lousse's nightie. By a brilliant sleight of hand we are shown the same situation from opposite directions: the narrating Molloy, sealed in his room, makes the adventures of his 'three-dimensional' counterpart seem as remote as the world through the wrong end of a telescope; while the Molloy character tries to make sense of the physical, temporal world without allowing for the fact that a mind as well as a body has a stake in what he does. Body, mind, and action provide suitable headings under which to examine this further.

Body

At Lousse's house Molloy's dissociation from his physical presence in the external world is no longer associated with social alienation (although Mrs Lousse's gaze plays a significant role), but with a conflict between alternative 'mappings' of the self. Self-estrangement now borrows the idiom of behaving 'out of character'. We are made aware that Molloy is the narrator's (fictional) creation but, in a way that typifies Beckett's ability, in drama or fiction, to use play on formal conventions as a means of refreshing our vision of human reality, we are given a sense of the mysterious relation between a person and his own physical attributes. The discontinuities in Molloy's actions are thus credited both to the narrator's fluctuating commitment to his character's consistency and to that sense of estrangement from one's own body that is so memorably rendered in Kafka's story 'Metamorphosis'. Enlarging on Molloy's inability to help bury Teddy, the narrator warns: 'si jamais cela m'arrive, oublieux de mon personnage, de me pencher ou de m'agenouiller, n'en croyez rien, ce ne sera pas moi, mais un autre' (p.47). However, a few pages further on, when Molloy does behave 'out of character' by exploring his room without the aid of crutches, the narrator archly explains, 'On ne se rappelle pas tout de suite qui on est au réveil' (p.50). In the context of his fictional world Molloy inclines towards a different sort of explanation and tends to attribute the peculiarities of his physical state to Lousse's interventions. He suspects her of adulterating his food with strange potions and blames 'les misérables molys de la Lousse' (p.72) for sudden leaps three feet in the air, or unaccountable collapses, even though for the reader these actions seem more characteristic of an ill-controlled string-puppet — or an author tired of his character.

Mind

When he observes the full moon outside his window, the time-span it implies conflicts with Molloy's sense of the passage of time since he saw its first quarter. Each time he examines his room it seems to have changed. Puzzles such as these lead Molloy to formulate a distinction between the outer world with its natural processes, and *his* world. He is led to suppose that his perceptions of the former belong to moments when he 'forgets' who he is and behaves as a stranger. Within the fiction this explanation helps him regain his customary indifference to the 'espiègleries de la nature' (p.55); but in a passage like the following it is seen to be an offshoot of the narrator's experience:

> Oui cela m'arrive et cela m'arrivera encore d'oublier qui je suis et d'évoluer devant moi à la manière d'un étranger. C'est alors que je vois le ciel différent de ce qu'il est et que la terre aussi revêt de fausses couleurs ... je glisse content dans la lumière des autres, celle qui jadis devait être la mienne, je ne dis pas le contraire, puis c'est l'angoisse du retour, je ne dirai pas où, je ne peux pas, à l'absence peut-être. (p.55)

If the baffling discontinuities of Molloy's experience are explained here by the narrator's oscillation between moments when he is restored, by proxy of Molloy, to the 'lumière des autres', and periods of what he tentatively calls 'absence' Molloy, too, will be credited with periods of oblivion:

> Oui, il m'arrivait d'oublier non seulement qui j'étais mais que j'étais, d'oublier d'être. Alors je n'étais plus cette boîte fermée, à laquelle je devais de m'être si bien con-servé, mais une cloison s'abattait et je me remplissais de racines et de tiges bien sages... (p.64)

In Lousse's garden Molloy, enjoying provisional respite from the anxiety induced by thought, seems to participate in the cycle of the seasons, the earth's rotation and the alternation of day and night, achieving an oceanic state which has as its counterpart a darker, more apocalyptic but still essentially cosmic dimension of the narrator's sense of his world.

The long excursus (pp.51-53) which interrupts Molloy's speculations about the moon is clearly of central importance in *Molloy*. In restrained, plangent tones of great poetic power, it communicates an extraordinary vision of human reality as a sort of alien planet. The passage begins comically enough with Molloy listing the sciences and disciplines in which he once dabbled in the hope that they would shed some light on the human phenomenon. He was fond of anthropology because of what he calls its 'puissance de négation, son acharnement à définir l'homme, à l'instar de Dieu, en termes de ce qu'il n'est pas'. The apophatic tradition in theology does indeed define God negatively, in terms of what He is not (i.e. human, finite, etc.), but if anthropology is not usually understood to extend this principle to man, Molloy and Beckett certainly do. The passage continues with an evocation of what the narrator calls 'mes décombres', an inner region depicted through images of ruin, imminent collapse, brittleness, empty wastes, murmurs, suspended movement: 'il paraît qu'ici rien ne bouge, ni ne bougera jamais, sauf moi, qui ne bouge plus quand j'y suis, mais regarde et me fais voir' (p.53). In fact one does not really go to or even see this place so much as *hear* it: 'C'est avec la tête qu'on l'entend, les oreilles n'y sont pour rien, et on ne peut l'arrêter, mais il s'arrête tout seul, quand il veut' (p.53); at the heart of our innerness is a fundamental otherness: Beckett's work ceaselessly finds images for this apprehension. We shall hear more of this sound in the last part of Molloy's narrative.

So if the narrator spends much of his time suspended between two kinds of oblivion, entailed respectively by losing himself in Molloy's activities and attending to his 'décombres', so Molloy spends much of his time in what he calls his 'boîte fermée' in a state of suspension:

La plupart du temps je restais dans ma boîte qui ne connaissait ni saisons ni jardins. Et ça valait mieux. Mais

> là-dedans il faut faire attention, se poser des questions ...
> Moi je me posais volontiers des questions, l'une après
> l'autre, rien que pour les contempler. Non, pas volontiers,
> par raison, afin de me croire toujours là. (p.65)

Thinking offers evidence of our existence: thus far Molloy
follows Descartes. But for Descartes, the gap between body and
mind leaves no room for a gap between the 'I' (the subject of the
cogito) and its thoughts: *Cogito ergo sum* is among other things
an affirmation of the sovereignty of the self. Not so for Molloy.
Thinking certainly reassures him that he exists (or that he is
'toujours là' as he puts it), but it situates him *between* his body
and his thoughts. In his 'boîte' Molloy not only contemplates
the body he knows to be his own, he also contemplates his
thoughts, perceptions and desires. If Molloy's thoughts tell him
that he exists they make it difficult for him to determine *where*
he exists.

Characterisations of thought as an essentially *divisive* activity
are especially abundant in this section of the novel. For example
Molloy tends to assimilate some types of thinking to a form of
(often defective) hearing. By playing on the ambiguity of the
words *entendement* and *résonner* ('to resound' but also a homo-
phone of *raisonner*), he represents thought not as an active
synthesising process but a passive, haphazard interaction
between disparate realms (pp.66, 82). Sight provides other
images. Noting that he has only one good eye he tells us that 'je
nommais difficilement ce qui s'y reflétait, souvent avec netteté
... je voyais le monde d'une manière exagérément formelle ... je
saisissais mal la distance qui me séparait de l'autre monde'
(p.66). The other world is of course simply the world outside the
mind with which Molloy finds it so difficult to enjoy any
consistent relationship. Lousse's house becomes an emblem of
rigid spatial and personal bearings with which the evidence of
Molloy's box-life rarely squares. At one point he observes:
'c'était moi qui n'étais pas assez naturel pour pouvoir m'insérer
avec aisance dans cet ordre de choses et en apprécier les finesses'
(p.58). A fine image of Molloy's inability to fit in with the
'natural' order — and a fine instance therefore of Beckett's

powerful vision of the strangeness of what it is to be human — is the description of the frilly nightdress Molloy finds himself wearing when he first wakes at Lousse's (p.61). Molloy's first morning at Lousse's house is, indeed, a delicious travesty of narratives such as Renoir's famous film *Boudu sauvé des eaux* which derive a comedy of failed rehabilitation from well-meaning attempts to reintroduce a tramp into the framework of social propriety.

Will

The whole of the Lousse episode, which covers a period of several months, is framed between Molloy's resolution to ask someone the name of the town he is in (p.40) and his abortive attempt to do so (p.83). Running over Lousse's dog foils the initial execution of this plan and Molloy wryly observes: 'En effet mes résolutions avaient ceci de particulier, qu'à peine prises il survenait un incident incompatible avec leur mise en œuvre' (p.41). The fact that Lousse does not fare any better by taking the precaution of keeping her dog on the pavement leads Molloy to coin a memorable maxim: 'Les précautions, c'est comme les résolutions, c'est à prendre avec précaution' (p.42). But obviously there is nothing very mysterious about the manifold contingencies to which our actions are subject. More perplexing (for Molloy) are the many things we do not do, despite an inclination or intention to do them: 'ne serait-on pas libre? C'est à examiner' (p.47). He reverts to the question of free will when he debates the issue of why he stayed so long with Lousse. Given the physical, empirical fact that he did stay, the only explanation he could give, he says, would inevitably end up proving that he could not have done otherwise. To explain this he cites a philosopher: 'j'avais aimé l'image de ce vieux Geulincx, mort jeune, qui m'accordait la liberté, sur le noir navire d'Ulysse, de me couler vers le levant sur le pont' (p.67). Ulysses's ship is sailing west, but the slave crawls eastwards and thereby exercises a paradoxical form of relative freedom within overall necessity, illustrating Geulincx's point that since mind and body are distinct realms, we have freedom only in the former while the

latter commits us to determinism. The point of Molloy's use of
the ship image is that it expresses his sense of a gulf between the
empirical fact that he did stay with Lousse and all the desires,
intentions and reasoning which might be adduced to explain this
fact. All the latter belong, he suggests, to a realm which has no
direct bearing on what he actually does, a realm in which he is
not leaving or going anywhere (p.67) notwithstanding his actual
movements. The point is not that there is no connection
whatsoever between desires and actions but that whatever
connection there is can neither be reduced to simple cause and
effect, nor effectively known. The issue is further clarified (or
obscured) in another connection. Noting that he occasionally
felt like looking for his bicycle, Molloy tells us that, 'cette envie,
au lieu d'essayer de lui donner satisfaction, je restais à la
contempler ... Car il semble y avoir deux façons de se comporter
en présence des envies, l'active et la contemplative, et
quoiqu'elles donnent le même résultat toutes les deux, c'est à la
deuxième qu'allaient mes préférences, question de tempérament
sans doute' (p.69). In what sense is the result the same whether
we translate a desire into action or refrain from doing so? What
Molloy implies is that, in this case, it is not the desire to find his
bicycle that will lead him to do so (or not), but purely haphazard, contingent circumstances. The dimension in which
bicycles are found or not found and the dimension in which
desires are formulated, contemplated, acted on (or not), may
overlap or coincide with one another but are nevertheless
distinct. And it is the fate of Molloy (and perhaps you and me)
to live simultaneously in, or rather between, these two
dimensions.

All this is mirrored by the distinction between Molloy's past
actions and their narration; indeed the retrospective narrator is
even more stringent and is inclined to frown upon the notion of
preference invoked earlier with regard to Molloy's attitude to
desires:

> Et quand je dis préférer par exemple, ou regretter, il ne
> faut pas supposer que j'optais pour le moindre mal, et
> l'adoptais, car ce serait une erreur. Mais, ne sachant

> exactement ce que je faisais ou évitais, je le faisais et évitais
> sans soupçonner qu'un jour, beaucoup plus tard, je serais
> obligé de revenir sur tous ces actes et omissions, pâlis et
> enjolivés par l'éloignement, pour les entraîner dans la
> pollution eudémoniste. (p.73)

Inherent in retrospective narration is the tendency to imply that,
where more than one possibility existed, an action was the
outcome of a rational, utilitarian choice between the alternatives, so that everything is dragged willy-nilly into 'la pollution
eudémoniste' (the S.O.E.D. defines *eudemonism* as 'that system
of ethics which finds the moral standard in the tendency of
actions to produce happiness'): narrative teleology always
threatens to impose coherence where none existed. Moreover,
the obsession with the relation between principles and experience
which is said to beset Molloy so frequently at Lousse's house, is
very much a preoccupation of the narrator's as he writes,
although his frequent allusions to the principles he is trying to
follow in his narration usually occur at the points where he is
aware of having departed from them. For example we are told,
in connection with another principle, that the narrator is
inclined to forget it, 'au même titre que si je ne l'avais jamais
dégagé' (p.60); but if this seems tantamount to acknowledging
that he is not really following any principles at all, what then
perplexes him is his sense that:

> quoi que je fasse, c'est-à-dire quoi que je dise, ce sera
> toujours en quelque sorte la même chose, oui, en quelque
> sorte. Et si je parle de principes, alors qu'il n'y en a pas, je
> n'y peux rien. Il doit y en avoir quelque part. Et si faire
> toujours la même chose en quelque sorte n'est pas la même
> chose que se conformer au même principe, je n'y peux rien
> non plus. D'ailleurs comment savoir si on s'y conforme ou
> non? (p.60)

Just as Molloy will end up doing the same thing (or some thing)
whether he acts on his desires or merely contemplates them, so
the narrator will end up saying the same thing (or some thing

which amounts to the same) whether he follows principles, breaks them or shuns them. It would be possible to infer a principle from any instance of behaviour, just as it would be possible to attribute it to a desire. But how, in any specific instance, is one to know if it genuinely conforms to a general law or only seems to? Seen in a wider perspective this brings us back to the relation between thought and reality, abstract and concrete, ratiocination and information, which, partly in connection with the question of principles, underlies the celebrated episode of Molloy's affair with the woman whose name was either Edith or Ruth (Molloy inclines to the latter name perhaps because of the Biblical echoes and the rude pun on the word 'rut').

For some reason the narrator thinks in retrospect that Lousse may have been a man 'ou tout au moins un androgyne' (p.75), and the story of Ruth stems from his attempt to justify this doubt about her sex on logical (or, in fact, totally illogical) grounds. The principles involved will turn out to be (approximately): if Molloy could have been mistaken once about the gender of someone he took to be a woman, the same might have been true the second time; and if the only women he has known were in fact men, the probability that Lousse was one as well would be high. But the Ruth episode involves a loftier principle, and a more painful doubt as well. As Molloy recalls it, the manner of his love-making with Ruth allowed for the possibility that she could have disguised her true sex from him. What distresses Molloy about this is the question which, in a rather less basic way, preoccupies Fabrice in *La Chartreuse de Parme*, namely whether or not he has known 'le vrai amour' (p.76). Here the conflict between empirical experience and mental abstraction is at its maximum. As Molloy heaps on the details, some sordid, some poignant, some hilarious, we may be inclined to think that his error is to suppose that when we speak of love what we have in mind are specific physical sensations. But Molloy (despite some of his more reckless outbursts: 'j'aurais fait l'amour avec une chèvre, pour connaître l'amour', p.76) is only too aware of the high spiritual and sentimental claims the human community has made for what it calls love; but how can he know whether he has experienced it? Grotesque as it is, the Ruth episode is narrated with the utmost vigour and comic resource. Perhaps its most brilliant feature is the way it subtly confuses and intermingles speculation around a purely empirical question (whether Ruth or Lousse was a woman or not) which could never be settled on entirely logical grounds with a purely subjective question (what do we mean by love?) which could never be settled on entirely empirical grounds. From hypothesis to hypothesis, from proviso to proviso, the human intelligence breaks like so many waves on the alien shore of reality. Progressively, *Molloy* imposes on the reader a memorable, and not merely sarcastic, image of man as the architect of frail but infinitely subtle patterns of thought, woven out of the profuse detail of experience. The changing status in the text of such patterns will be considered in the next section.

No explicit connection is made between Molloy's finally leaving Lousse's house and the quest for his mother (although the Ruth passage is accompanied by renewed references to her which mainly concern Molloy's comic — and archly pseudo-Freudian — efforts to deny the shameful fact that he tends to confuse Mother, Lousse, and Ruth). When he leaves it is apparently at the instigation of an inner voice: 'la petite voix qui disait, Barre-toi, Molloy, prends tes béquilles et barre-toi' (p.79). Leaving Lousse's house is neither one of those haphazard actions which retrospective ('eudemonistic') interpretation would betray; nor does it arise within the framework of contemplated desires and inclinations where, as regards staying in or leaving places, Molloy was inclined to indulge his contradictory impulses alternately (see the passage on the 'deux pitres', p.64). The voice which abruptly tells Molloy to leave has no apparent antecedents, except, of course, the sudden impulses to see his mother. We shall have occasion to consider it again in the last section of Molloy's narrative to which I will now turn.

MOLLOY'S REGION

If Molloy's movements seem to be determined by the wax and wane of his desire to see his mother, this fluctuation seems itself to stem from the incompatibility between seeking her and finding her, and between finding her and settling what he now calls 'cette affaire entre ma mère et moi' (p.86). It now seems that it is not purely inadvertently, but when 'la nature de cette affaire perdait de la consistence, pour moi, sans toutefois se dissiper entièrement' that Molloy tends to move away from the geographical location in which she might be found. But he is never outside the orbit of the quest for his mother, which does not really belong to geographical space.

On leaving Lousse, Molloy finds himself in 'un autre monde' (p.80), a regulated universe where 'tout se tient' (p.83). However, his way of orienting himself in and his attitude to what is simply the ordinary world soon betray his inconsistency with its Leibnitzian 'harmonie préétablie', and he quickly super-imposes on it the haphazard coordinates of what he now repeatedly refers to as 'ma région'. Having considered, then rejected, the notion that his region has any specific limits, he tells us:

> Je préférais m'en tenir à ma simple croyance, celle qui me disait, Molloy, ta région est d'une grande étendue, tu n'en es jamais sorti et tu n'en sortiras jamais. Et où que tu erres, entre ses lointaines limites, ce sera toujours la même chose, très précisément. (p.88)

In the remainder of his narrative, Molloy will not enter the town again, but will find himself in some of the further reaches of his region: the sea-shore marked by images of clarity and infinity, and the forest where images of obscurity and finality will predominate. One set of oppositions and tensions therefore drops out of the narrative, as Molloy's consistency with his surroundings increases. But it is replaced by another conflict which has until now been, so to speak, camouflaged by the others: a conflict between motion, progress, movement, and arrival, achievement, finality. This conflict, which will hence-forth dominate Molloy's narrative, is in direct continuity with the narrator's situation, to which the passage I quoted switches abruptly:

> Mais à présent je n'erre plus, nulle part, et même je ne
> bouge presque pas, et pourtant rien n'est changé. Et les
> confins de ma chambre, de mon lit, de mon corps, sont
> aussi loin de moi que ceux de ma région, du temps de ma
> splendeur. Et le cycle continue, cahotant, dans une Egypte
> sans bornes, sans enfant et sans mère. (p.88)

This is the beginning of a passage which ends with the words
'Fin du rappel', and implements an intention declared by the
narrator a few pages earlier: 'Ainsi de temps en temps je
rappellerai mon existence actuelle dont celle que je conte ne peut
donner qu'une faible idée' (p.82). The point of these interventions is sometimes, as in the present case, to suggest a link
between Molloy's interminable journey and the narrator's sense
that what he calls his own journey ('ma course', pp.80, 110) is
not yet over. At a number of points in the narration (pp.17, 60,
109) he alludes to his presentiment of a future moment when he
will have to draw up an inventory of his possessions. Until such
a moment comes he must avoid the temptation to give a
definitive summary of any aspect of his existence.

The parallel with Molloy's desire to settle once and for all the
outstanding matter with his mother is never forced on the reader
but slowly imposes itself on him in the last portion of the
narrative. Presently we shall have to examine the link between
Molloy's rapidly decelerating progress and physical deterioration in the forest, and the narrator's desire to reach the kind of
plateau from which he would like to survey his existence. But
first I should like to turn to the area of thought and consider the
way in which the opposition between open-ended fluidity and
definitive closure figures in some of the discursive passages of
the narration.

Thinking is never a very happy or satisfying business in
Molloy; it is all too often addressed to a role to which it is at
once destined and, apparently, ill-suited — that of introducing
discursive order into the chaotic realm of experience. Like most
of Beckett's protagonists, Molloy is equipped with a distinctly
analytical mind which constantly pits itself against his profound
conviction that experience is incomprehensible. In the last

portion of the narrative, however, there is less occasion for the
baffled perplexity encountered earlier. Instead there are a
number of passages where, in different ways, thinking is
channelled in such a way as to diminish the injuries it is inclined
to inflict on the certainty and coherence at which it aims. Two
supreme but divergent examples are the passage on the knife-rest
Molloy purloins from Lousse's house and the celebrated passage
concerning Molloy's attempt to find a satisfactory solution to a
problem involving the pebbles he is fond of sucking. The
passage about the knife-rest is anticipated to some extent by a
remark Molloy makes early in the narrative: 'Ramener le silence
c'est le rôle des objets' (p.16). The burden of this remark is confirmed from time to time when Molloy is, for example, tempted
to interrupt his narration by the description of his bicycle, or its
horn: 'Parler de bicyclettes et de cornes, quel repos' (p.20). The
point about the knife-rest, however, is that Molloy has no idea
what it is (nor may the reader until the same object crops up at
Moran's house, p.157) and is never likely to find out. It is therefore accessible and tangible, whilst at the same time infinitely
mysterious. Having described it in scrupulous detail Molloy
observes:

> Je pouvais donc l'interroger sans fin et sans danger. Car ne
> rien savoir, ce n'est rien, ne rien vouloir savoir non plus,
> mais ne rien pouvoir savoir, savoir ne rien pouvoir savoir,
> voilà par où passe la paix, dans l'âme du chercheur
> incurieux. C'est alors que la vraie division commence, de
> vingt-deux par sept par exemple et que les cahiers
> s'emplissent des vrais chiffres enfin. (p.85)

From Molloy's point of view the beauty of this object is that
although, in common with most of the things to which he
addresses his mind, it both invites and resists interpretation, the
knife-rest like the symbol of pi with its recurring decimal does
not pretend to be reducible to sense and finitude, given that
Molloy excludes the possibility of ever knowing for sure what it
is.

The moral of Molloy's epic quest (pp.92-100) for an equitable distribution of sucking-stones is, in the end, the same. But the quest seems initially motivated by a desire to set local order and harmony against chaos and infinity, and to restore a sense of 'mesure' which Molloy feels has been losing considerable ground 'depuis le temps que je me débattais dans cette histoire' (p.95). The result, of course, is the opposite. The more Molloy ponders the merits and defects of various systems which occur to him, the more it appears that formal perfection is incompatible with the complexity of human needs (p.99). But in any case the conflict only exists at a theoretical level since he realises that, in practice, 'je me moquais éperdument de me sentir en déséquilibre ... comme cela m'était parfaitement égal aussi de sucer chaque fois une pierre différente' (p.100). It would seem, however, that such futile and irrelevant calculations have their benign aspect. For, in the framework of the narration, they belong to a period of alleviation and repose. To worry about pebbles is a relief from other worries. And, for the narrator, to adopt the pedantic tone which characterises this episode, is evidently to find a sort of relief from his anxieties.

Having stressed how desirable, convenient and appropriate it would have been for him to stay in the forest, Molloy notes

> Mais je ne pouvais pas, rester dans la forêt je veux dire, cela ne m'était pas loisible. C'est-à-dire que j'aurais pu, physiquement rien ne m'eût été plus facile, mais je n'étais pas tout à fait qu'un physique, et j'aurais eu le sentiment, en restant dans la forêt, de passer outre à un impératif.
>
> (p.116)

His account of such imperatives puts a new complexion on many aspects of his narrative. Among their principal characteristics is the fact that they all bear on the question of his mother, that although Molloy is always inclined to comply with them they never lead him anywhere, and that, ultimately, they are super-fluous since they merely underline what is in any case a 'dis-position permanente' on his part. In fact what he calls his imperatives, and the voice which bears them, merely serve to highlight the contradiction between his present circumstances and any kind of finality.

By assimilating his impulses to action with the promptings of an inner voice, Molloy might seem to be drawing attention to a hidden source, a primal, unconscious motive, which intermittently asserts itself. But the voice, in its peremptory, rhetorical fashion, only seems to undermine what it purports to motivate (p.117). What is primal is the fact of motion itself; Molloy's imperatives serve only to provide a short-lived justification and orientation for what is prior to and, ultimately, alien to them. If they spring from a source extraneous to his usual cogitations, this simply reflects the fact that 'sorting something out with one's mother', like waiting for Godot, is no more than the intermittent content and aim given to an inherently open and aimless state. Immediately after the passage on imperatives the narrator interrupts an account of Molloy's thoughts with the following qualifications:

> Oh je ne me tenais pas ce limpide langage ... Et chaque fois que je dis, je me disais telle et telle chose, ou que je parle d'une voix interne me disant, Molloy, et puis une belle phrase plus ou moins claire et simple ... je ne fais que me plier aux exigences d'une convention qui veut qu'on mente ou qu'on se taise. Car c'est tout autrement que les choses se passaient ... En fait je ne disais rien du tout, mais j'entendais une rumeur, quelque chose de changé dans le silence, et j'y prêtais l'oreille ... il y avait simplement quelque chose de changé quelque part, qui faisait que moi aussi je devais changer, afin que rien ne fût changé (pp.118-19).

If Molloy's movements keep him at a fixed distance from any destination, his thoughts insulate him from any perception of change or progress. This latest version of the relation between Molloy's 'thought' and 'reality', between his progress and any goal, effectively eliminates any residual distance between character and narrator. Their positions are now more or less identical: Molloy's region is the same as the narrator's. The narration has brought Molloy to a point where his movements in physical space are a betrayal rather than a clarification of the narrator's circumstances. But to remove Molloy entirely from the physical world would be to remove him from the sphere of representation. The achievement of a total convergence between Molloy's story and the narrator's circumstances would involve clarification of the relation between the sense of having experience in an external world and the sense of existing in the disembodied dimension of one's consciousness. In the face of this the narration, simulating a conclusiveness it cannot achieve, seems to adopt the solution of more or less arbitrarily introducing Molloy into an atmosphere of purely artificial finality. Let us examine the constituents of this synthetic image of an end.

First, of course, there is the progressive decline of Molloy's bodily faculties. The arbitrariness of this decline manifests itself most clearly perhaps in the way Molloy, as he minutely itemises his various deficiencies, and their effect on his progress, places himself in the position of a spectator, celebrating the superiority of 'la démarche du béquillard' (p.85) or the advantages of 'la reptation' (p.120), or adopting the guise of an independent witness expertly adjudicating between various forms of apparent misfortune. The discrepancy, frequently alluded to by the narrator, between Molloy's seemingly invincible constitution, 'ma santé qui ... était au fond d'une robustesse inouïe' (p.109), and his physical infirmities also underlines the paradoxical status of his bodily decline.

Secondly, images of death figure prominently in the last pages of Molloy's narrative. But they too take a form which undermines the sense of finality they imply. His inability to conceive of any definitive extinction (p.91) leads to a tendency to conceive death as a kind of subterranean continuation of life: the notion of being buried alive occurs on one or two occasions (pp.35, 47). And his desultory reflections on, or attempts at suicide (e.g. p.82) tend to culminate in his uncertainty as to whether death is as final as it seems.

Thirdly, there is Molloy in the forest. Towards the end (pp.118-24) it is as if he were in a kind of tomb. Everything is enveloped in shadow (the word 'noir' is insistently repeated) and

has the consistency of dense metals. The sky is 'plombé' (p.120);
the leaves which are 'immobiles et raides' make no noise as they
fall; 'on aurait dit du laiton' (p.121). The temperature is uni-
form. Molloy can scarcely hear his bicycle horn and cannot hear
the 'murmures' of the forest but only the distant sound of a
gong which he mistakes at first for the beating of his own heart.
What is Molloy's relation to this environment? At one level it
seems to act as a reflection of his sense that this is his last chance
to reach his mother since he will soon not be able to move at all.
But at the same time Molloy's progress, slow as it is, is in
opposition to the forest's terminal atmosphere. And indeed it is
when he reaches its edge and finds himself in a ditch bordering
the grassy plain across which he can just discern the outline of a
town that he finds himself incapable of further progress. Both
Molloy's presentiment that he would one day gaze at the plain
(p.115) and the conviction, noted the previous time he found
himself in a ditch, that 'j'y reviendrai sans doute un jour, ou
dans une dépression analogue' (p.35) are confirmed. But the
ditch is now a border between an environment (the forest) in
which he cannot reach his goal but on which he can get some
kind of grip — he pulls himself along by using his crutches as
grappling-hooks; and a dimension (the plain) which denies progress: 'Comment me traîner à travers ce vaste herbage, où mes
béquilles tâtonneraient en vain?' (p.123), but in which Molloy's
goal is (or may be) located. The incompatibility of Molloy's
journey and its goal seems at this point to have achieved its
clearest, and most mythic, formulation. And yet, no sooner has
Molloy taken cognisance of a situation which he had in any case
anticipated, than the voice which usually dictates his imperatives
comes to his aid again: 'Je m'entendis dire de ne pas me biler,
qu'on courait à mon secours. Textuellement ... Ne te bile pas,
Molloy, on arrive' (p.123). The colloquialism of this intimation
is a comic travesty of the earlier imperative which had
culminated in grave and learned Latin: 'nimis sero' (p.117): it
thus further heightens the grossly artificial nature of the last
portion of Molloy's narrative.

The boundary which Molloy has reached is, as much as anything, the frontier between the fictional world he inhabits and

the realm which is its source — that of the narrator. What the narrative seeks to resolve is the narrator's divorce from what he calls his mother's room: it aims to transform a hypothetical, speculative and purely accidental location into one grounded in ontological necessity. The rich connotations of the phrase 'la chambre de ma mère' — unity with the mother, the womb, an anterior, primal state of belonging — suggest that it denotes a place the narrator is exiled from rather than where he is. If the narrator could reconcile his sense of existing in a spaceless, timeless vacuum with his sense of a coherent sequence of events in the empirical world, Molloy's narrative could bring him to his mother's room. It is the impossibility of this reconciliation that keeps Molloy's progress in three-dimensional space, and the narrator's quest for an end, evolving in parallel with one another. The maternal room is, in a sense, the infinity at which parallel lines meet.

In trying to reconcile the two dimensions the narrator succeeds only in superimposing the discontinuities inherent in his own circumstances on to those which characterise Molloy's experience, and in making the fiction a travesty of the narration. The arbitrary and artificial elements which I have pointed to in the last segment stem from the increasing pressure which the narration exerts on the narrative. The shadowy silence of the forest with its unreal sounds is perhaps no more than a transparent disguise for the darkened room in which the narrator lies. And Molloy's rapid physical decline brings him ultimately to the immobility which is the narrator's state. All this stems from the narrator's attempt to bring the narrative to some conclusion: 'Et maintenant, finissons' (p.121). But if he succeeds in making some sort of an end it is at the cost of a double failure. On the one hand he has transformed Molloy into a kind of mythical creature and on the other hand he is obliged to end the narrative on a note of flagrant contradiction: Molloy has been brought to a halt, but since, despite his transmogrification, the narrator has been unable to make him either arrive or expire, the story must somehow continue. The last sentence: 'Molloy pouvait rester, là ou il était', plays beautifully on the ambiguity of this situation by begging the question of where Molloy is: is he *out there* in the story, or *back here* — where he has always been — at the story's origin, on its eternal threshold? From here only another story can begin, but perhaps out there, in the realm of stories, someone *will* come and fetch Molloy.

3. Incarnations: Moran

Every time I read *Molloy* I look forward to the opening of section two. No longer surprised to find, as I embark on the second half of the novel, that the narrator is now someone calling himself Jacques Moran, I nevertheless still derive pleasure from the sudden switch of tone, idiom and narrative persona; if anything the pleasure is enhanced by anticipation.

The story Moran tells is in essence simple. It is a fable of disintegration and metamorphosis, an account of events that totally transformed his life: having been sent out to find Molloy, he succeeded only in losing himself. The parallel with Molloy's quest for his mother is obvious, and the circumstances in which Moran writes are also reminiscent of Molloy's in some respects: he writes, ostensibly at least, for others (a report commissioned by his employer) and in the context of a present which is shapeless and indefinite. But the relationship between moment of writing and past events differs. In Molloy's narrative, as we saw, the status of the 'event' is undermined from the outset, and throughout, by the narrative mode. This is not true to anything like the same extent in Moran's case. While the status of the representation will *eventually* be subject to a similar degree of indeterminacy there is much less local interference: the 'mise en question' of the narrative by its own processes is not conducted in anything like as piecemeal a fashion. Stylistically, too, Moran's narrative is less dense than Molloy's, and the paragraph divisions make it easier to read.

But if the tale Moran tells is more self-sufficient than Molloy's it is also exposed in a larger measure to a kind of undermining which springs from the sense that the story one is reading is an ironic reflection of stories one has already read. It is possible to identify various interacting levels of parody involving the story's overall pattern, some of its local features and details, and the way it is told. Moran gives us a species of 'récit initiatique': a first-hand retrospective account of experiences that led to radical change in an individual's perception of himself and the world. Most of the staple ingredients of such narratives are here — the sudden breakdown of routine, the sense of foreboding, the feeling that 'things will never be the same again', the enhanced appreciation of all one has hitherto taken for granted, the sense of being drawn into a strange and unfamiliar world, the feeling of personal fragmentation and a related upheaval in one's relationship with familiars, and so on. But here all these things are laid on so thick and are so evidently one-dimensional that they become caricatures of themselves. In some of its details, too, Moran's story caricatures literary genres and sub-genres and even specific texts. His visit to Father Ambroise bears more than a passing resemblance to the famous scene in *Madame Bovary* where Emma goes to see the Abbé Bournisien in search of spiritual support and receives only the most humdrum pseudo-medical advice, of the 'keep on taking the pills' variety. There are clear offshoots of Kafka in the details of Moran's profession and enigmatic employer, but here they are grafted on to a framework that is more reminiscent of Sherlock Holmes; the 'perilous' journey into the 'Molloy' country seems occasionally to wink at the adventure story *à la* Stevenson, and some of the descriptions of his transformation have an air of Jekyll and Hyde and other narratives concerned with the often unwelcome discovery of 'another side' of one's nature; Moran's paternalism often has a Victorian ring reminiscent of the critical and satirical portraits of fathers to be found in Butler or Gosse. Then there is Moran's style as a narrator: in the foreground, of course, the peevish, pedantic, self-important tone which makes him in many respects a brilliantly funny caricature of petit-bourgeois values and provincial narrow-mindedness. But in the midst of all the smug 'opinions', the proprietorial complacency, is a disconcerting element of self-parody, a self-conscious recognition of one's own fatuousness. This is partly, of course, a function of the 'before and after' structure: the Moran who writes can no longer take his past self seriously. But Moran's narrative does not really allow for such a clear-cut division: it is evident that he 'now' lacks any sense of an alternative self to pit against his past one, and therefore what he registers most consistently is his awareness of a gap between the self and all its manifestations. Even in his presentation of the past, Moran, as we shall see, tends to make us constantly aware of this division. All these elements of parody undermine Moran's story and by giving it a self-conscious, self-critical dimension prevent us from taking it at face value.

In the remainder of this chapter I shall offer a selective commentary on the main phases of Moran's tale, emphasising the fable and its parodic aspects and leaving other factors — the narratorial interventions and the relation with Molloy's narrative — to be considered at the end.

THE INNER AND THE OUTER

Moran's narrative falls into two roughly equal portions, the first covering a period of just over twelve hours between the summons to seek Molloy and Moran's departure; the second his journey and eventual return, a period of about a year. In the first half Moran reports meticulously on the disastrous effect the anticipation of his quest has on the habitual order and calm of his everyday life. Rapidly we become aware that his ordered universe, far from being a natural extension of himself, is the product of strenuous efforts to suppress or conceal latent disorder: his world of principles, habits and possessions is fissured by contradictions which begin to show through the moment he is obliged to address his mind to Molloy. The most prominent opposition, initially, is between outward appearance and inner disposition. Moran likes to think of himself as a creature of externals, 'un solide parmi d'autres solides' (p.137), and to regard others as consistent with the way they seem. Ironically, he is perfectly aware that he is himself far from what he appears to be and that others — his son, his servant Marthe, the local priest Father Ambroise — are far from what he wants them to be. The stability of his world depends, however, on his ability to force others to confirm the self-image he cultivates and to conform to the image he wishes to have of them.

One of the many roles Moran plays in the elaborate social comedy he has perfected is that of a practising Catholic of moderately liberal views. Work and play, he opines, are permissible on the sabbath as long as one's 'état d'esprit' befits a Sunday. Nevertheless, when Gaber arrives dressed in black, 'lourdement endimanché', Moran is irritated by what he takes to be a 'grossière observance de façade, alors que l'âme exulte en ses haillons' (p.127). By making him miss the 12 o'clock mass, Gaber does not, however, jeopardise Moran's spiritual life so much as the scrupulous regularity on which his role depends. Moran is exposed to the ridicule of his free-thinking neighbour (p.132) and, when he seeks to repair the damage by seeking a private appointment with Father Ambroise, to the suspicions he suspects the priest of harbouring.

Moran's interview with Father Ambroise is a masterpiece of black comedy. Two interconnected themes are prominent: the ironic interference between spiritual and bodily needs and the opposition between outer and inner dispositions. Before setting off for the church, Moran wonders if the priest will be able to tell that he has drunk lager before taking communion: 'M'accorderait-on le corps du Christ après un pot de Wallenstein?' (p.131). God, in any case, will know sooner or later. Moran, who is usually precise in his meal-times and a hearty eater, is obliged to postpone his Sunday lunch. But throughout his session with Father Ambroise the idiom of eating — the gratification of physical hunger — becomes confused with the taking of the host from which Moran expects the spiritual equivalent of a good meal. Having received communion he observes: 'Je n'aspirais qu'à une chose, regagner mon domicile le plus vite possible et m'empiffrer de stew. L'âme assouvie j'avais la dent' (p.137). At home he finds the stew disappointing and suspects Marthe of having omitted the onions just as he had wondered if Father Ambroise had slipped him unconsecrated bread.

Moran's desire to foster an image of himself is reflected in the upbringing of his son and namesake Jacques. He wants his son to resemble what he appears to be rather then what he knows he is, and he justifies paternal cruelty on the familiar grounds that he wishes his parents had spared him bad habits by exercising greater firmness (p.130). The image of paternal authority which permeates Moran's narrative has theological overtones. His most characteristic habit is his desire to check and spy (imitating God's supervision of the universe) while himself remaining inscrutable.

Moran finds it impossible to think of Molloy without withdrawing into the darkness of his bedroom; here he can locate Molloy in an elemental realm where individual existence surrenders to archetypes.

> C'était seulement en le déplaçant dans cette atmosphère, comment dire, de finalité sans fin, pourquoi pas, que j'osais considérer le travail à exécuter … J'aurais prêté à mon bonhomme, dès le début, des allures d'être fabuleux.
>
> (p.151)

The Molloy he evokes in his imagination (pp.153-54) is by no means inconsistent with the figure in the earlier narrative, but the purely external viewpoint does indeed make him seem like some strange creature of fable:

> Qu'un homme comme moi, si méticuleux et calme dans l'ensemble … créature de sa maison, de son jardin … qu'un homme ainsi fabriqué, car j'étais une fabrication, se laisse hanter et posséder par des chimères, cela aurait dû me paraître étrange. (p.155)

One of the striking things about this passage is Moran's acknowledgement that he is (or was), as he puts it, a 'fabrication' (the English version has 'contraption'): everything from his proprietorial spirit to his rationalism, from his religious faith to his chickens, is carefully cultivated to suppress what now, in the shape of his vision of Molloy, threatens to overwhelm him. Moran's world does not reflect his inclinations, it is designed to conceal them; all his habits have a prophylactic function and his principles are not derived from convictions but from a desire to exorcise uncertainty.

When Moran asks himself questions about the peculiar organisation in which he is employed he finds that very little of it withstands logical scrutiny: it seems as implausible to him as it does to the reader (pp.144-46). But the commands of Youdi (his 'employer'), which are always formulated in the prophetic future tense, have one main feature: it is unthinkable for Moran to disobey them. As in the case of Molloy's imperatives, the stimulus to action always seems to come from outside the habitual framework of will and desire but, since its external nature cannot truly be identified, it merely tends to accentuate the contradictory status of the individual. When Moran recalls Gaber's summary of his task he is perplexed by two seemingly incompatible features. The stipulation that his son must accompany him seems to accentuate its external, practical and contingent aspects. Yet he cannot recall any reference to what he is supposed to do with Molloy when he finds him. This gives his mission an inherent indeterminacy: the missing detail, like Molloy's imprecision about what he wants to settle with his mother, marks the inherently irrational and contradictory status of Moran's journey.

Since it is only by withdrawing it from the plane of action that he can give his mission any substance, it is hardly surprising that Moran's elaborate preparations regarding transport, equipment and clothing are totally arbitrary. As he prevaricates, he alludes repeatedly to the collapse of his customary control and urbanity: 'Je perdais la tête déjà' (p.168); causes for vexation abound. But Moran encounters resistance, and engenders chaos, only when asserting the sovereignty of his will and attempting to remain in the world of the father. All goes sweetly, on the other hand, when (as in the case of his ludicrously impractical outfit) principles are disregarded and Moran's preparations are attuned to the 'atmosphère ... de finalité sans fin' (p.151) in which he locates Molloy. Moran's initial decision to travel by moped elicits this comment: 'Ainsi s'inscrivait, au seuil de l'affaire Molloy, le funeste principe du plaisir' (p.134), a sly allusion to Freud's notion of two conflicting principles working on the ego, the pleasure principle associated with instinctual drives and the reality principle associated with repression and rationality. I shall consider presently the significance of such allusions to Freud.

TO BALLYBA AND BACK

Moran's increasing estrangement from the world of actions is accentuated, once he has embarked on his journey, by the difficulty he now has in communicating his wishes unambiguously to his son. This culminates in the hilarious *quid pro quo*s over the bicycle (pp.194-96). Transplanted from the ground of domestic life, paternal authority loses its basis in an apparently natural order of principle and begins to function in a vacuum.

The three-day period Moran spends alone (pp.197-210) has a structural role comparable to Molloy's sojourn with Lousse: the protagonist ceases to be in transit and stands in a particularly passive relationship to the various disjointed elements of his experience which are represented in a paradigmatic form. In his makeshift shelter Moran unsuccessfully attempts to concentrate on the question of Molloy. The first time he drags himself to a nearby stream; having disturbed the water 'j'attendis que mon image se reconstituât, je la regardais qui tremblante me ressemblait de plus en plus. De temps en temps une goutte, tombant de mon image dessus, la brouillait à nouveau' (p.198) — a powerful image of self-estrangement. On the next occasion, seeking to identify 'ce qu'il y avait de changé depuis quelque temps en moi' (p.202) Moran finds that only metaphors will do: 'ces pauvres figures, où sans doute mon sentiment de débâcle cherchait à se contenir' (ibid.) — *figures* is apt since it is often in terms of an altered visage or countenance that Moran attempts to pin down the process of self-dispersal in the grip of which he finds himself. Images of subsidence and collapse predominate: 'ce que je voyais ressemblait plutôt à un émiettement, à un effondrement rageur de tout ce qui depuis toujours me protégeait de ce que depuis toujours j'étais condamné à être' (ibid.). Having lost all fixity, the self becomes assimilated to a formless space which resists all but 'apophatic' definition — in terms of what it is not.

Towards the end of his first day alone Moran is visited by someone who has features in common with Molloy and with the man Molloy called B (he has a sort of club, p.198). On the second day Moran assassinates another man who both resembles him physically ('même petite moustache ratée, même petits yeux de furet, même paraphimosis du nez ...', p.205) and who also claims to be in pursuit of a 'Molloy' figure. Together these scenes, notable for their high degree of artificiality, reproduce a number of elements from Molloy's narrative and accentuate Moran's dissociation from earlier images of himself (including that of someone with a purpose). But they do so in a way which amusingly caricatures the conventions ('symbol-laden' atmosphere, element of ritual, etc.) in which such archetypal encounters are usually based. When Jacques returns with a bicycle Moran plays the role of parent and pedagogue for the last time. He gives the orders, his son pedals, the bicycle transports them. For the father the journey is largely mental, for the son purely physical; the incongruity of an empirical journey towards an impalpable destination is underlined. After several weeks they arrive in Ballyba.

In its utter ordinariness and ease of access Ballyba is totally unmysterious, and this of course makes the parody of mysterious lands all the more evident, and adds to the amusingly discordant effects created by Moran's earlier pseudo-Balzacian excursus on the local toponymic conventions — regions take the name of their principal town but add the suffix *ba* (p.182). In the few days between his son's final departure and Gaber's sudden reappearance (p.221) Moran enjoys a reprieve from the grip of purpose, aware that its duration is determined by the extent of his provisions and by the 'logical' necessity that 'something' will happen (we encountered this in Molloy's narrative when narration exerted its pressure). Fear of Youdi's sanctions still inspires 'd'enfantins espoirs' but Moran dismisses them (p.220). Like Molloy in his last ditch Moran can see the lights of a town in the distance. Initially he identifies affectionately with them: 'les braves petites lumières des hommes' (p.217); but he soon finds them risible: 'sales petites lumières clignotantes d'hommes terrifiés' (p.220).

Now and then Moran thinks about himself: 'Et quant à moi, ce passe-temps fidèle, je dois dire que je ne pensais guère à lui': the amusing play on pronouns vividly renders Moran's self-dissociation as do these further reflections: 'Mais par moments il me semblait que je n'en étais plus très loin, que je m'en approchais comme la grève de la vague qui s'enfle et blanchit, figure je dois dire peu appropriée à ma situation, qui était plutôt celle de la merde qui attend la chasse d'eau' (p.221). Thus Moran discourages himself — and the reader — from conceiving his evolution in terms of accession to a more authentic order of selfhood. What Moran feels closer to is not a self in the sense of any kind of consistent entity, still less the 'fundamental core of his being' or what have you, but, rather, to an experience of self-scattering and fragmentation prior to any kind of identity. Earlier in the same paragraph Moran sarcastically dismisses the notion that his journey to Molloy's region involved the revelation of some sort of primal zone of being by a play on the Freudian term libido — the alleged source of instinctual drives: 'Et cet Obidil, dont j'ai failli parler, que j'aurai tellement voulu voir de près, et bien je ne le vis jamais, ni de près, ni de loin et il n'existerait pas que j'en serais que modérément saisi' (p.220). Fabulous creatures — the Obidil, Molloy, the self — are the hunter's hardest game because, in all probability, they do not exist.

Gaber's sudden reappearance with the instruction to return home confronts Moran with exactly the same conundrum as the instruction to find Molloy — the problem of having to reconcile mutually incompatible images of human existence. The implausible Gaber is still the messenger of a fixed, eternal order from which Moran feels excluded, but by a clever reversal this order is now associated with 'ordinary' humanity. To reassure Moran that Youdi has not changed, Gaber cites one of the master's recent, homely apophthegms: 'Il m'a dit, dit Gaber, Gaber, qu'il m'a dit, la vie est une bien belle chose, Gaber, une chose inouïe' (p.221). At this, Moran, closing his eyes to evade Gaber's infuriating smile, enquires, 'Vous croyez qu'il parlait de la vie humaine?' The name *Youdi*, as some commentators have pointed out, can be read as an imperative, a corruption of *You do*. For Moran he generally seems to represent the origin and the hypothetical stimulus of one's actions. Youdi's fluctuations (like Godot's) — from secular 'patron' (p.146), to Godlike issuer of categorical commandments formulated in the future imperative (*You will*), to homespun philosopher, 'human all too human' — clearly mirror Moran's changing experiences and reorientations, reflecting different theorisations of what it is that keeps him going. Youdi is always the reflection of a theory about man, an anthropology; and by this stage Youdi is nothing else but the sheer fact of human existence itself with no teleological perspective. As such, 'Youdi''s commands are no less compelling: Moran must 'go on', carry on, 'go home'; but Moran has now to recognise that the source of his actions — the imperatives to which he responds — are internal to him, and at this point in his narrative Youdi becomes assimilated to, or rather displaced by, a voice which is within Moran.

Moran neatly divides the matters that concerned him on his way back into two categories: mind and body. The first category is subdivided: there are the two sets of questions he fruitlessly pondered, and then, more gratifyingly, the thoughts about his bees. The hilarious list of sixteen 'questions d'ordre théologique' (p.226) expressed in a mixture of scholastic and argotic idioms is placed on the same level as the seventeen questions 'qui me touchaient peut-être de plus près' (p.227) which relate directly to his circumstances and erstwhile familiars. The world of Zoulou and the Elsner sisters, of Moran's chickens, of the Youdi whose office is reputedly 'au 8 square des Acacias', is now as remote and unreal as the 'monde frivole et charmant' of medieval scholasticism in which it makes sense to ask what God was doing before the Creation or whether one should approve 'le cordonnier italien Lovat qui, s'étant châtré, se crucifia' (p.227). To make any sense, theological conundrums presuppose a powerful body of belief. The same is true of Moran's questions about his circumstances: without a framework of reliable assumptions about man they are senseless. Now lacking such a framework, Moran turns with relief to thoughts of his bees. He is fascinated by the complex sign-language through which bees communicate with each other by varying the angle of their flight and the pitch of their hum (Moran evidently has some inkling of this, but unlike Beckett he does not appear to be familiar with Von Frisch's classic work on the subject which seeks to explain it all). For the point of Moran's investigations is not scientific mastery. Indeed his delight springs from the conviction that his hypotheses could never lead to definitive knowledge and from his sense that while the bees' dance, like Molloy's knife-rest, admits of infinite interpretations, it sanctions none. As he explains in a passage which rings ironically with the self-assured cadences of classical prose, what Moran now enjoys in his contemplation of the bees' dance is the way it affronts human reason and man's remorseless, self-serving, anthropomorphism: 'Ce serait toujours une chose belle à regarder et d'une portée que n'arriveraient jamais à souiller mes raisonnements d'homme malgré lui. Et je ne saurais faire à mes abeilles le tort que j'avais fait à mon Dieu, à qui on m'avait appris à prêter mes colères, mes craintes et désirs, et jusqu'à mon corps' (p.230). Contemplating the bees, and, later, attuning himself to the bird-song in his garden, Moran — 'l'homme malgré lui' — seeks to wean himself of the images he had once craved. Images of reversal, trespass and death dominate the last few pages. Skirting the cemetery, Moran reaches his old wicket-gate; finding that his key will not open it, he smashes it down (p.236). Moran is now a trespasser on his own land, an intruder in his own house, a survivor of his own dissolution, simultaneously dead and alive. The latter notion had figured earlier in Moran's pride at his 'concession à perpétuité' in the local cemetery; but for ecclesiastical disapproval it would already have borne the legend 'ci-gît' followed by his name and birthdate. Passing it on his return Moran perversely adapts Youdi's maxim about life: 'C'est beau d'avoir une concession à perpétuité. C'est une bien belle chose. S'il n'y avait que cette perpétuité-là' (p.236). The paradoxical blend of perpetuity and moribundity, of death in life and life in death, alert us, as they did in Molloy's narrative, that we are close to the frontier between the fiction and the circumstances in which it originates. But before turning to consider fully the signs of Moran writing in his room, I want to take stock of the story he has told us.

THE DISFIGURED SELF

With its neat, circular plot, its particularised and yet still generic figures, its thematic consistency, Moran's narrative has the trappings of a fable — a tale that demonstrates a point. The story not only embodies images of considerable scope and power, but develops and pursues some of their ramifications; it builds up for example a complex network of social conformity, religious orthodoxy, family relations, habits, possessions and opinions, at the centre of which are images of authority and tradition vested in the figure of the father. And it presents us with admirably diverse, shifting, always provisional imagery of inner collapse and disintegration. Now, it seems clear that, as a fable, Moran's story involves a shift from one of these poles to the other, a progressive and seemingly irreversible mutation out of the realm of the former into the grip of the latter. But what kind of sense does the fable make of this transition? On what system of understanding is it seen to be based? In a very general way the answer seems straightforward: Moran falls under the sway of that great twentieth-century model of inwardness, the unconscious: 'an allegory of the psyche's discovery of its own depths' would be one way of encapsulating this aspect of the tale.

Yet it is in this very area that caricature and parody are at their most vigorous. Where we might expect at least a modicum of discrimination and nuance we are given the whole caboodle: the text is littered with the bric à brac of modern myths of the self, the unconscious is served up with all its trimmings — Youdi, the Obidil, Molloy, the pleasure principle, antithetical selves, animus and anima, narcissism, family relations, pansexualism, fetishism — in a mish-mash which suggests all kinds of connections but validates none. And, not surprisingly, these bits and pieces of psychoanalytical lore lack all cohesiveness: no alternative version of selfhood can be recuperated from them except perhaps the essentially negative and — to risk overusing the word — apophatic one, which is reflected in the unstable figures Moran keeps devising to communicate his experience and to spurn and scoff at more positive representations. In Moran's narrative, parody wreaks its greatest havoc on the visions of selfhood by which we set greatest store, be it the sovereign self of one who thinks he is master in his own house, or the inner self to which the introspective tradition from Montaigne to Freud invites us to lay claim. If Moran the man of property, with his Micawberish relish for the advertisement of principle ('Quand je peux faire plaisir, sans faire violence à mes principes, je le fais volontiers', p.142), has his comeuppance, so does the Moran who, however fleetingly, is tempted to pin his faith on alternative, more authentic and organic visions of the self such as those by which the modern psychologist might flatter us.

As a fable the core of Moran's story involves the progressive withdrawal from available representations of human existence. As he slowly drifts out of their reach, the only substitutes he can find are outside the human sphere. But his final phase — in the garden of his own house, his untended bees reduced to a friable ball that crumbles in his hand (*boule* echoes the passage (p.202) where this word had designated Moran's own dissolving image) — is no more than a stop-gap. Moran seeks to inure himself to meaninglessness by foregoing human language and attempting to attune himself to birdsong (p.237), but this is only a pastoral-primitive variation on the self's old themes. If it conveys admirably what one might term Moran's *anthropophobia* — his desire for severance from recognised figurations of man's estate — it also underlines the seeming impossibility of escaping from the realm of images. If the fable ends with Moran re-entering his house to take up his pen, the desire to cast off once and for all from human moorings ('Je ne supporterai plus d'être un homme, je n'essaierai plus. Je n'allumerai plus cette lampe', p.238) conflicts with the need to report on and disentangle himself from the past. Moran will find himself (or *has* already found: by the time we reach this point we have already read the ostensible product of this decision) confronted with the ineradicably divided, contradictory nature of the human being: both an image and that which repulses images, both a past and a present, an inside and an outside, a something and a nothing. If the fable constantly undermines and never resolves its own movement towards a more satisfying visualisation of the self it is not only because it lampoons and ironises its own basis as a fable but also because it tends increasingly, as it progresses, to refer the reader to its own origins — a level at which it is not so much a story producing meanings as the product of a story-telling process.

LISTENING AND WRITING

Moran's narrative is ostensibly a report on recent experience and is written in circumstances which ensued: after a spell in the garden he is revisited by Gaber who commissions a report on Youdi's behalf, Father Ambroise calls round, his son returns, Moran sits down to write... But, interspersed with this apparent resurrection of the 'old order', we are given another version: while in the garden Moran attunes himself to the voice he had heard on his return and, in response to it, he goes back into the house to write: 'C'est elle [la voix] qui m'a dit de faire le rapport' (p.238). The discrepancy between these two versions obviously reiterates divisions which marked the closing stages of Moran's journey (the substitution of the voice for Youdi), but here it is seen to offer alternative accounts of the origin of the fable itself: on the one hand a commissioned report on the past, written in compliance with external criteria, on the other a potentially free response ('Est-ce à dire que je suis plus libre maintenant?', p.239) to an inner call. Moreover the discrepancy is further intensified by the fact that the last words of the narrative — 'Alors je rentrai dans la maison et j'écrivis. Il est minuit. La pluie fouette les vitres. Il n'était pas minuit. Il ne pleuvait pas' (p.239) — categorically deny it the status of a report. Not only does this underline the problematic nature of the relationship beween the fable and the circumstances in which it is written, but, in referring us back to the text's opening — 'Il est minuit. La pluie fouette les vitres', etc. (p.125) — it also invites us to consider both the fable and the account of its origins as belonging to the order of fiction. With this in mind, let us now look at the scattered references to the moment of writing in Moran's narrative.

In the opening paragraphs the act of writing is implicitly attributed to two different origins: the obligation to compile a report for Youdi, and a more general compulsion to write associated with a sense of being 'done for' ('Je suis fichu', p.125). Thereafter the most prominent interpolation in the early pages is the passage where Moran informs us that he is not sure whether statements about his general inclinations or tastes hold good at the time of writing: as a precaution he will use the past tense as much as possible. Later, however, Moran renders this distinction otiose:

Car en écrivant cette journée je suis à nouveau celui qui la subit, qui la bourra d'une vie anxieuse et futile, dans le seul but de s'étourdir, de pouvoir ne pas faire ce qu'il avait à faire. Et ainsi qu'alors ma pensée se refusait à Molloy, de même cette nuit ma plume. Il y a quelque temps que cette confession me travaille. Elle ne me soulage pas. (p.165)

Narrative and narration confront, evade and react against the same problems and obstacles.

This, of course, still maintains a distinction between *then* and *now* even if it suggests that it might be hard to disentangle them. However, scattered sporadically, and more concentratedly towards the end, we come across interpolations which, like many of those in Molloy's narration, suggest either that the details which give the fictional world its substance are purely arbitrary or underline, in some way, the subordination of representation to narration. Here are some examples:

1. 'J'ai menti en disant que j'avais des dindes, etc. Je n'avais que quelques poules' (p.173).

2. 'Je ... pris ma gibecière, j'ai failli écrire ma guitare' (p.171).

3. 'D'où Ballyba tirait-il donc son opulence? Je vais vous le dire. Non, je ne dirai rien. Rien' (p.183).

4. 'Je ne raconterai pas mon raisonnement. Cela me serait pourtant facile. Il aboutit à la décision permettant la

composition du passage suivant' (p.191).

  5. 'Si j'avais entendu parler d'autres oiseaux qui crient et
chantent la nuit, je les aurais écoutés également' (p.207).

  6. 'Car m'étant réveillé à nouveau vers l'aube, cette fois
sous l'effet d'un besoin naturel, et la verge en légère érection,
pour plus de vraisemblance, je ne pus me lever' (p.189).

In a number of ways, not necessarily consistent with one
another, such interventions tend to discredit the events Moran is
reporting. If he writes about owls, nightingales and corncrakes it
is because he has heard *of* them, rather than because he heard
them. If he writes *gibecière* rather than *guitare* it is because it is
more plausible that he should have taken a bag than a musical
instrument. But why should Moran be concerned with plausibility or verisimilitude or coherence? This amounts to asking
why he writes at all. And one answer to that question is that he
writes for Youdi. But it is not the complete answer, as Moran
reveals in a long digression approximately a third of the way
through his narrative. Compliance with Youdi's commission is,
Moran tells us, only the apparent reason why he writes:

> Et ce triste travail de clerc qui n'est pas de mon ressort, je
> m'y soumets pour des raisons qui ne sont pas celles qu'on
> pourrait croire. J'obéis encore aux ordres, si l'on veut,
> mais ce n'est plus la crainte qui m'inspire. Si, j'ai toujours
> peur, mais c'est plutôt là un effet de l'habitude. Et la voix
> que j'écoute je n'ai pas eu besoin de Gaber pour me la
> transmettre. Car elle est en moi et elle m'exhorte à être
> jusqu'au bout le fidèle serviteur que j'ai toujours été,
> d'une cause qui n'est pas la mienne. (p.179)

To recognise that Youdi is no more than the external pretext
for what he does is to acknowledge a much more radical dissociation; it is to be the 'fidèle serviteur ... d'une cause qui n'est
pas la mienne' but which is not Youdi's either; as he writes,
Moran acts at the behest of no authority other than his own even
if he does not recognise this authority as his. Such a recognition
involves a double dissociation: it poses a powerful threat to

Moran's attempt to identify himself with the stereotyped roles he has cultivated, but at the same time it fails to sanction any alternative, private image of himself since the voice is inherently impersonal. As he writes, Moran fears that the voice will be the agency of a permanent expropriation from 'les absurdes douceurs de mon intérieur, où chaque chose a sa place, où j'ai tout ce qu'il faut sous la main pour pouvoir endurer d'être un homme' (p.180).

Let me now try and draw out some of the implications of this. Moran's narratorial interventions undermine the representation in various ways, not least by drawing attention to the context of narration itself. If this is obviously very reminiscent of Molloy's narrative there are, nevertheless, significant differences. In Molloy's case, it will be remembered, the effect is to create a hierarchical relationship between narration and representation, the latter being, so to speak, discredited the more one recognises the ascendancy of the former. The reader is drawn to envisage everything in the text as a reflection of the narrative situation and a product of the narrative process. But in Moran's case the effect is not really to create a hierarchy but, firstly, to place narration and representation on the *same* level as different planes of a fiction and, secondly, to locate the originating impulse of the fiction outside both these planes. The obsessive image of the *voice* — which comes to dominate both the sphere of representation (Moran hears it on his way home; it supplants Youdi) and that of narration (Moran responds to it as he writes) — tends to make the narrational context as much a part of the fiction as the rest:

> Comme vous voyez, c'est une voix assez ambiguë et qui n'est pas toujours facile à suivre, dans ses raisonnements et décrets. Mais je la suis néanmoins, plus ou moins, je la suis en ce sens, que je la comprends, et en ce sens que je lui obéis ... Elle me dit aussi, cette voix que je commence seulement à connaître, que le souvenir de ce travail soigneusement exécuté jusqu'au bout m'aidera à supporter les longues affres de la liberté et du vagabondage.
> (pp.179-80)

If they occur in the context of narration, allusions to the voice tend to refer us (as they do at the end of this passage) to the representation. The same is true, *mutatis mutandis*, the other way round: in the context of representation they refer us to narration. The only factor tending to pull us out of this circular process is the sense that the voice is extraneous and anterior to both these levels of the text. In either sphere it is regarded as something that is paradoxically both an origin (without it Moran couldn't do anything) and a distant goal (Moran thinks he will need to tune into it more and more). Not only is this very reminiscent of the thematics of voice in Molloy's narrative, it also emphasises the fact that, in manifold ways, it is *to* Molloy's narrative that we are constantly drawn as we read Moran's. Now one way of looking at this is to say that Moran 'turns into' Molloy (in the passage just quoted, the 'longues affres de la liberté et du vagabondage' anticipated by Moran *do* sound reminiscent of Molloy's journey). But it makes more sense, I think, if we take it that we are led back to Molloy's narrative as the origin of Moran's rather than as its sequel.

The first thing one can point to in support of this reading is the nature of the parallel that exists between the two narrators' situations. Moran's circumstances not only echo Molloy's on many points of detail (writing for an employer, feeling 'done for', etc.), they are like a distorted mirror image. But here there *is* a distinct hierarchy. However implausible it is, the *mise en scène* of Molloy's situation as narrator is tied to a complex inter-action between past and present, inner and outer, here and there. The equivalent in Moran's case has, by comparison, a distinctly perfunctory and offhand quality about it; like his fable, Moran's circumstances as a writer are more transparently fictional and 'story-like' than Molloy's and moreover, unlike Molloy's, they are explicitly 'revealed' to be no more than a fiction by the last words of the novel as a whole. What I think the reader is asked to recognise, then, is that the two narratives which make up *Molloy* are linked not by connections at the level of the fiction but by the fact that they must in the end be attributed to a single narrator who adopts successive disguises, travestying himself in various ways. A couple of passages in

Moran's narrative leave little room for doubt on this score, and even add further, potentially infinite, ramifications:

> Oh je pourrais vous raconter des histoires, si j'étais tranquille. Quelle tourbe dans ma tête, quelle galerie de crevés. Murphy, Watt, Yerk, Mercier et tant d'autres. Je n'aurais pas cru que — si, je le crois volontiers. Des histoires, des histoires. Je n'ai pas su les raconter. Je n'aurai pas su raconter celle-ci. (p.187)

This seems to take it for granted, so to speak, that 'Moran' is no more than the temporary disguise of an anguished, and presumably anonymous, storyteller who could just as well have told us about, and incarnated himself as, Murphy or Watt or Yerk or Mercier (Molloy's name is tantalisingly omitted from this list but does appear on a similar one on page 228). But by a further twist the list of names refers us to none other then Samuel Beckett himself, author of *Murphy*, *Watt*, *Mercier et Camier*. Of course we already know that Samuel Beckett is in one sense the 'author' of Moran's narrative but this is in a dimension of authorship from which the book's narration remains hermetically sealed: no amount of circumstantial evidence can alter the distance and distinction between Samuel Beckett the Irish author and the narrator of *Molloy*. But if the narrator of *Molloy* is not Samuel Beckett, he is not, it seems, Moran or Molloy either. It is not Moran who imagines a story about Molloy or Molloy who imagines Moran. Rather 'Molloy' and 'Moran' are figments of a single imagination, fragments of one shattered identity implicit in but never directly presented in the book: a man in a room thinking, remembering, imagining, creating, above all, perhaps, writing. To pursue this is of course to look at *Molloy* as a whole and to move, however tentatively, towards some general conclusions.

4. Beyond 'Molloy'

'Que voulez-vous, on est ce qu'on est,
en partie tout au moins' (p.71).

To recognise that the two narratives in *Molloy* have a common origin within the text is not to find an answer to a problem but to have one's sense of the problem revised. This process of revision on the reader's part is, I think, crucial to the book's effect. We need, it seems, to have a sense of the difference between Molloy and Moran, to envisage them as variegated identities susceptible to change, and to construe the one's quest for the other in terms of levels of personality, depths of experience, degrees of alienation and authenticity. But we then need to feel this ground shift under us or, changing the metaphor, we need to feel this carpet — with its familiar patterns — slipped from under our feet as we recognise more or less belatedly that the real action of the novel, in the terms I used at the end of chapter 2, is not *out there* in the story but *back here* in the narration — where stories start. What is involved is a potential and necessarily gradual transformation in the reader's perception of the text which is likely to come about through an increasing awareness of two dimensions of narration. Firstly, the substance and texture of the narratorial discourse as it manifests itself word by word. Secondly, the handling of narrative levels which distributes, allocates and channels discourse between various personae and positions. In this concluding chapter I shall examine these two facets in turn, stressing their respective roles in the constitution (or destruction) of visions of selfhood.

LANGUAGE, DISCOURSE AND INTERTEXTUALITY

Molloy is one of those books which makes us acutely aware of language, not just *its* language but language itself. This is true of all Beckett's fiction (and of *Ulysses* and *A la recherche*, too): 'In the beginning was the pun', proclaims *Murphy*. But while Beckett's previous novel, *Watt*, was essentially concerned with *reference*, the general relationship of language to what lies outside it, and while the trilogy inaugurated by *Molloy* will home in with ever greater insistence on the problematic relationship of language and selfhood — on what it is like to feel that one is 'en mots ... fait de mots, des mots des autres' (*9*, p.166) — *Molloy* gives us a comparatively wide-angled view on the spectacle of language. It occurs frequently, for example, as a specific theme, especially in the first narrative where diatribes against the expressive (in)capacities of words abound. But over and above its presence as a theme, language in *Molloy* confronts and intrigues the reader from the outset in the form of discourse, the dimension in which language is considered not so much as a tool but as a medium in which human subjectivity is reflected.

The world of *Molloy* is first and foremost one of discourse, or *discourses*. The plural is appropriate not because two discursive territories are labelled 'Molloy' and 'Moran', but precisely because despite the factors which individualise these 'characters' their narratives are remarkably alike and manifest the same general — and plural — qualities: unstable, multi-faceted, carrying many channels (mythic, philosophical, comic, vernacular, highbrow, Gallic, Anglo-Irish etc.). And yet, by another twist, all these discourses find a precarious (or hypothetical) unity in the text which weaves them together, and in the shadowy narrative persona of the weaver, so that we feel a tension between the singular discourse *of* the text and the multiple discourses *in* it. In focussing now on the latter, I want first of all to stress the richness and diversity of the fictional discourse Beckett creates in *Molloy* by rapidly enumerating some of the principal features and effects (they have cropped up piecemeal in preceding chapters), and I shall then treat in more detail one particular device — intertextual allusion — which has hitherto received less attention.

The first category in which some of these effects can be grouped is *self-conscious narration*: the use, familiar enough in modern fiction, of a narrator who is not only deemed to be the author of the book we are reading but who also comments regularly on the process of composing it. The Beckett narrator in *Molloy* is self-conscious to a degree which has few precedents since the eighteenth century.[9] The more obvious types of narratorial intervention — interruptions, digressions, bifurcations, commentary — are massively present; and so are many other often more conspicuous ones. For example:

1) Sudden grammatical breaks which leave a sentence dangling in mid-air, e.g.: 'Mais un homme à plus forte raison moi, ça ne fait pas partie des caractéristiques d'un chemin, car. Je veux dire que ...' (p.12).

2) Constant qualification using phrases such as 'C'est-à-dire'.

3) Interjections bearing on the discourse itself, of the 'yes, that's it' variety (e.g. the anaphoric use of *oui* and *mais* in pages 10-20, *mais* occurring no less than twenty-five times, often at the beginning of sentences).

4) Repetition of words, indicating a pause for thought on the narrator's part: 'La chambre sentait l'ammoniaque, oh pas que l'ammoniaque, mais l'ammoniaque, l'ammoniaque' (p.22).

5) Breaks in syntax indicating switches of direction, doubt: 'Je ne — je ne me sentais pas malheureux' (p.26), 'Je — non, je ne peux pas le dire' (p.23).

6) Constant invocations of the reader, direct: 'Oh pas des notions comme les vôtres ...' (p.91), or indirect, 'Je le sais, je le sais, ne me fatiguez pas' (p.32).

7) Commentary on specific features of discourse: 'C'est là une façon elliptique de parler' (p.25), 'Récrire tout cela au plus-que-parfait' (p.20), 'Je parle au présent, il est si facile de parler au présent, quand il s'agit du passé. C'est le présent mythologique, n'y faites pas attention' (p.33).

8) Obtrusive verbal patterning, especially symmetry, e.g. the sequence 'D'ailleurs, je ne venais pas pour l'écouter' (p.22), '... pour l'argent' (p.23), 'Mais ... pour l'argent' (p.24).

9) Textual rhythms often leading to crescendos, e.g. the sequence culminating in 'Alors crions, c'est censé faire du bien'

[9] See Robert Alter, *Partial Magic: The Novel as Self-Conscious Genre*, Berkeley: California U.P., 1975.

(p.33), or in 'Ne pas vouloir dire, ne pas savoir ...' etc. (p.85).

10) Multi-lingual and multifaceted vocabulary, incorporating neologisms: *acatène* (p.19), *trasciner* (p.77); rare and specialised words: *eudémoniste* (p.74), *podex* (p.226), peculiar expressions: 'à l'homo mensura il faut du staffage' (p.84).[10]

All these devices intensify the self-consciousness of the narration and tend, in addition, to create a pervasive sense of artifice. As such they foster a further kind of effect which can be roughly categorised as *textual autonomy*.

By this term I mean the feeling that the text is somehow producing its own energy, that it is to some degree self-generating and autotelic. Wordplay, so rife in *Molloy*, is a major factor in this respect. Puns such as this: '... la bonne ville, celle qui m'avait donné la nuit' (p.24) (instead of 'le jour'); or this: 'le destin me réservait à une autre fosse que celle d'aisance' (p.47), are very frequent. Taken individually they would perhaps simply serve to characterise the narrator as someone highly conscious of words, and given to sardonic, often scatological, humour. But some wordplay is more disruptive. In an early passage Molloy, having remarked that his mother was 'sourd comme un pot' (p.21) immediately follows this up with a run of cloacal references which seems to have been so to speak set off by the ambiguity of the word *pot*. It is at such moments that we are given the uneasy feeling, referred to in a preceding chapter, that what we are reading is purely arbitrary; and the eerie sense that there is 'no-one there' behind the text and nothing ahead of it except blank space to be filled at the instigation of words. This species of textual autonomy works in conjunction with another which occurs at moments when literary conventions seem to be the principal determinants of narrative incident or episode, as if the text's main concern were not to report on something pre-existent or independent but to 'keep up appearances', to main-

---

[10] This curious maxim combines the Latin tag *homo mensura omnium* ('man the measure of all things') with a neologism formed from the word 'staff', presumably in the musical sense of 'stave'. Man needs to see himself as a fixed entity against which to measure the things he orders. *Staffage* seems, mockingly, to assimilate human order to a commodity, like roughage, of which man needs a regular intake.

tain an illusion of verisimilitude. Much of the 'plot' of the two
narratives, with their constant tendency to travesty, could be
viewed in this light. But it is especially in the field of narration,
at points when the narrators seem particularly diffident about
their endeavours — when Molloy for example follows up the
explanatory phrase, 'si vous voulez', with the sardonic, 'moi je
veux bien' (p.47), as if to tell the reader that he can have the
story any way he wants it — that the arbitrariness of stories is
given its full force. On such occasions the order of narrative in
its very gratuitousness and irrelevance becomes representative of
any order or explanatory system (including language itself), and
the effect of such moments is to reveal a double fracture between
the narrator and his discourse: at the level of experience, as if to
say 'It wasn't like that at all, those explanatory systems don't
fit', and at the level of narration, as if to say 'These words
betray me, I am not saying what I want to say'. At such points
the text threatens to break down entirely (hence the frequent
ellipses, signs of fluster and so on enumerated above). In order
to avert the threat it must patch up its differences, make its
peace with the order of narrative discourse, rehabilitate itself by
resuming, sometimes with amusingly weary heavy-handedness,
the 'pensum' of coherent composition. Continuity is achieved
with the aid of familiars: the comedy of maladjustment, the
pathos of metamorphosis and psychopathology, the wry accents
of baffled perplexity at the oddities of volition and perception —
in short the mythic and philosophical dimensions of the text,
always there to save the narrative and to give it substance, but
always, too, beside the point.

My third category is *intertextuality*. *Molloy* is teeming with
the discourses of western culture; it mixes styles, registers, tones,
combines the French language with English idioms and Irish
references, engenders anachronism, and creates an overall effect
of displacement. Intertextual effects have a prominent role here
(in this context I mean by intertextuality the way in which one
text or discourse — including social or political ideology —
crops up and inhabits another). *Molloy* is littered with bits and
pieces of Cartesianism, Scholastics, myth, and cultural
reference, which create a network of intertexts the principal

effect of which is simultaneously to adumbrate and to disqualify (often by mutual incompatibility) potential sources of meaning and explanation. Many instances of this effect have been commented on, but here I want to consider a slightly different kind of intertextual function. In a discourse as in-growing as Molloy's, seemingly so remote, too, from specific social or historical context, one effect that intertextuality can achieve is the sudden invasion of the text by aspects of reality one had imagined bracketed out. I shall examine two instances of this.

The first occurs in one of several passages where Molloy expresses a vision of men in society as a violent, blood-thirsty, vengeful mob anxious to eradicate anything that threatens its order (pp.89-90). At one point he offers advice on the best times of day to avoid being the victim of the human race in its rage for order. Worst is morning when humans are 'assoiffés d'ordre, de beauté et de justice'. In late afternoon one needs to watch out for 'les vigiles' who work at night. But night itself is not so bad, we are told, 'Car l'épuration qui s'y poursuit est assurée par des techniciens, pour la plupart. Ils ne font que ça, le gros de la population n'y participe pas, préférant dormir, toutes choses considérées' (p.90). The measured language intensifies the fierce irony, but part of the irony is intertextual: certain key words, primarily *épuration*, but also *vigiles*, have powerful historical resonances. The unsettled period following the liberation of Paris from German occupation has come to be known as the *épuration* because of the backlash against those who had collaborated. Many were officially brought to trial but unofficial violence was also widespread. Newspapers were full of accounts of well-organised gangs roaming town and country districts settling old scores (many having little to do with the occupation).[11] In the context of Molloy's narrative the word *épuration* triggers a number of responses. It suddenly introduces a specific context — the historical realities of the period when Beckett was writing — but without acknowledging it as such; it therefore reminds us of the book as artifact: author com-

[11] For a historical account see Robert Aron, *Histoire de l'épuration*, 3 vols, Paris: Fayard, 1967-74; and for a fictional one see Simone de Beauvoir's *Les Mandarins*.

municates with reader above the head, so to speak, of his narrator. But it also helps to ground the issues (and values) hovering in the text at this point in a reality outside the book, and hence to articulate, as part of that generalised astonishment at what human beings are which so permeates the novel, a profound sense of shock at the Hobbesian ferocity of the human animal.

My second example also involves the post-war period; this time cultural discourse, and specifically the ideas of Albert Camus, provide the intertext. Moran, about to embark on his account of the journey to Ballyba, takes stock of his intentions in writing. At the core of a particularly intricate paragraph which turns on the dialectic (so pervasive in *Molloy*) of experiencing and narrating, Moran suddenly introduces the figure of Sisyphus in order to make a comparison. Whereas, he notes, a 'doctrine en vogue' (evidently the one expressed in Camus's *Le Mythe de Sisyphe*, published in 1941) has it that Sisyphus experiences a fixed succession of emotions as he eternally rolls his rock, exulting at the top of the slope, lamenting at the bottom, Moran wonders if Sisyphus really cares anyway; or if he possibly keeps thinking that each rolling will be the last, so that 'Cela l'entretiendrait dans l'espoir, n'est-ce pas, l'espoir qui est la disposition infernale par excellence, contrairement à ce qu'on a pu croire jusqu'à nos jours' (p.181). Here Moran echoes Camus very closely indeed, and apparently with approval. Camus does argue that hope is an affliction which severs us from the existential facts of life and prevents us from embracing life in its relativity (like Sisyphus).[12] But the sort of humanistic affirmation which informs Camus's repudiation of hope is not what Moran has in mind, as he makes clear in his concluding flourish, asserting that whilst hope of change *would* be awful, 'se voir récidiver sans fin, cela vous remplit d'aise'. The implication seems to be that recognising that there is no real point in distinguishing living and telling, then and now, yesterday and tomorrow, far from confirming man's Promethean possibilities — his capacity to make something

[12] Camus put the case against hope most pithily in one of his early essays: 'l'espoir, au contraire de ce qu'on croit, équivaut à la résignation. Et vivre c'est ne pas se résigner', *Noces*, Paris: Gallimard, Coll. Folio, 1972, p.49.

positive out of his condition as long as he faces it squarely —
confirms that life is a repetitious joke. Through the intertextual
reference some of the tenets of existentialist humanism are
acknowledged but kept at a distance. Moran's casual phrase
'une doctrine en vogue' suggests both the doctrinal aspects of
Camus's thought, and its widespread appeal, two factors which,
it is implied, reveal its relatively superficial apprehension of
what it is to be human. Through this and other scattered
references the philosophical discourses of Beckett's own period
inhabit the text in the same way as Cartesian metaphysics,
empiricism and scholasticism: as arcane systematisations with
little grip on reality.

A prime characteristic of the modernist works to which
Beckett had been so responsive was their highly intertextual
nature, sometimes characterised as their 'allusiveness'; Eliot,
Pound, Apollinaire, Yeats, Joyce would all be obvious
examples. 'Allusion' stemmed from the author's sense of a lack
of cohesive explanatory systems (Christianity or science, for
example) and its function was twofold: to reflect fragmentation
by using fragmentation itself, but also, crucially, to make the
fragments themselves cohere, to weld something together out of
them, by making analogies and creating new myths. Graham
Hough sums this up admirably in a discussion of the modernist
lyric. 'Classical culture', he writes, 'has lost its unique
authority',

> The poet has all the myths of the world available to him;
> which also means that he has none — none that can impose
> itself as indubitably his own by simple right of inheritance.
> The one inevitable unifying intellectual force in the
> modern world is that of natural science; and since the poet
> is concerned with areas of experience that natural science
> does not touch, he is left to make his own myth, or to select
> one by an arbitrary existentialist choice, from the vast
> uncodified museum, the limitless junk-shop of the past.[13]

[13] 'The Modernist Lyric' in Malcolm Bradbury and James McFarlane (eds),
Modernism, Penguin, 1976, p.316.

In Beckett's fiction what is stressed is the arbitrariness; here intertextuality is not allusive; it is centripetal rather than centrifugal. But if, in a new dispensation, sometimes called 'postmodernist', writers as diverse as the *nouveaux romanciers* in France, American fabulators such as Pynchon, Barth and Gass, outsiders like Borges and Gombrowicz, have created fictions which, in various ways, revel in the endless arbitrary profusion of representation, taking more or less for granted that the literary text is master in its own house, Beckett's name should not be too hastily allied with theirs. In his texts there is really no euphoric relinquishing of the bonds between the textual and the existential (even if gestures in this direction are part of his narrators' stock in trade); nor, in the end, is there any attempt to instil new forms of consciousness, appropriate to a lucidly ludic vision. And there is none of that sense of conversion from one set of values (those of realism surrendering to the cult of subjectivity) to another (the cult of, and then the repudiation of, subjectivity) which marks in some ways those works we associate with modernism or post-modernism. Neither allusive nor euphoric, intertextuality in Beckett's fictions serves a double role. By keeping resonant some of the voices of Western culture it helps to maintain, as powerful options, the claims of the individual subject to external mirrorings of itself, to a selfhood ontologically grounded. But at the same time it helps to undermine these claims, in their legitimacy and in their efficacy, by manifesting itself, through the texts' fictional structures, as a process rooted in the workings of reflexive consciousness itself. Beckett's fictions are haunted by a sense that the mind's quintessential mode is citation: in quest of the source of its own authority, it can only cite alien authorities. When it wishes to play the author, it finds that it can only quote.

NEW MYTHS FOR OLD?

By a wonderful *tour de force* two fictional structures compete with one another in *Molloy*. The first would foster a mythic grasp of human experience: a myth of alienation, metamorphosis, exile, uncomfortable certainly, but also comforting in its confirmation that the human mind — the artist — can get some kind of grasp on the human condition and, through such images as these, show us what we are. But this structure — and the vision it promotes — is wholly subordinate to another, which encloses it. And this second structure, in its deployment of narrative levels, forces us to conceive of the mythic consciousness as something produced within the text by certain pressures and desires in the authorial subjectivity which lies behind, but is not to be confused with, Molloy and Moran.

And yet it is perfectly legitimate to ask if this elaborate structure does not itself facilitate the creation of another myth, particularly when we consider subsequent novels, *Malone meurt* and *L'Innommable*, which not only give us further ramifications of the same fictional structure but pursue specific, alternative, options already present in *Molloy*. A brief look beyond its compass will help to focus these questions about *Molloy*.

In *Malone meurt* the narrator presents himself as aged, bed-ridden and determined, above all, on filling the time that remains to him in a way that will minimise the burden of self-consciousness. His strategy is to tell himself stories which he hopes have as little bearing as possible on himself. But in this he has little success as his stories constantly betray his own concerns, becoming thinly-veiled autobiography or breaking down altogether: 'Tout est prétexte, Sapo et les oiseaux, Moll, les paysans, ceux qui dans les villes se cherchent et se fuient, mes doutes qui ne m'intéressent pas, ma situation ...' (*8*, p.171). But in the later parts of the book, Malone does manage to plunge himself into a magnificent, fierce story which is designed to end in the annihilation of all its characters; and ostensibly he does contrive to die in the telling since we are invited to surmise that the book's last words are also his last. But when we pick up *L'Innommable*, Malone has himself been relegated to the status of a figure in a story: 'Malone est là. De sa vivacité mortelle il ne reste que peu de traces ... Mais il sera peu question de Malone, de qui il n'y a plus rien à attendre' (*9*, p.9).

For the narrator of *L'Innommable* takes the opposite tack: he wants to get out of this 'enfer d'histoires' (*9*, p.155) and to purge himself of surrogates such as Malone — and Moran, Molloy,

Murphy... All these are denounced as stand-ins, gross caricatures which have usurped his place and wasted his time by
luring him, by their proxy, to conceive of himself in *their* terms,
that is in terms which make selfhood a matter of relation to an
external world: 'Pourquoi me suis-je fait représenter', he asks
himself, 'parmi les hommes, dans la lumière?' (*9*, p.17). But if
the self cannot be represented in these terms, can it be
represented at all? Beautifully crafted, *L'Innommable* initially
articulates a purely negative vision (admirably summed up in the
title of one of Beckett's best late plays: *Pas moi*): a coruscating
verbal assault on one's own imaginings of selfhood, a
repudiation of 'pantins' (*9*, p.8), 'ces souffre-douleur' (*9*, p.28),
'mes homuncules' (*9*, p.32), 'moribonds' (*9*, p.36), 'importuns'
(*9*, p.80), 'bagnards' (*9*, p.86), 'transfuges' (*9*, p.156), 'paquets
de sciure' (*9*, p.173), etc. But as the text develops, another
thread, ever-present, becomes increasingly intertwined: the
hypothesis that behind (or at the origin of) all these avatars is an
'I' whose advent will follow their banishment. And this second
'movement' is followed by a third where the continuing
denunciation of all pretenders, even those initially more con-
genial figurations of self spawned in the onward rush of the
narrator's discourse, is accompanied by a sense that the real
strangers in whose midst the narrator vainly seeks himself are
words themselves: 'Je suis en mots, je suis fait de mots ... tous
ces étrangers, cette poussière de verbe, sans fond où se poser,
sans ciel où se dissiper' (*9*, p.166). In a manner anticipated and
annotated throughout the trilogy, language, in its mediation and
generality, affirms itself as antithetical to selfhood.

On the basis of what I have outlined it would seem reasonable
to judge *L'Innommable* to be a more radical text than *Molloy*,
purer and more schematic in its structure, more specific and
graver in its diagnoses. And yet all readers of the novel will
probably recall that the seemingly relentless concessions of
defeat to language's dominion are accompanied by the equally
relentless affirmations, on the part of the 'I' which enunciates in
written or spoken form, that however remote and distortive it
finds its own utterances it *must*, by dint of the very criteria by
which it repudiates those utterances — and the cargo of images

they carry — in some sense be distinct from them. And to that extent 'It' must be deemed to exist, even if only on logical grounds, or in the manner of the apophatic God. As it proceeds, the text engenders ambiguity with regard to the status of the hypothetical 'I' seemingly affirmed in and through the proliferation of the text itself. And the question arises of whether this 'I' is yet another figment, language's equivalent of a *trompe-l'œil* effect, a purely formal entity entailed by the structure of language (verbs must have a subject, subjects must have predicates, I must have an I ...), or whether it is to be considered an originating nucleus of individuated life. The copresence of these alternatives is crucial to the text and the ambiguity is certainly not resolved but reduplicates itself at other levels, and primarily in the form of uncertainty as to the force which drives the text: is it simply discourse itself in its tendency to self-proliferation and generativity (factors as potent here as in *Molloy*); or is it life-affirming human stoicism, a refusal to be vanquished, a commitment to going on — forces which would in themselves constitute a certain kind of self in the self-affirmation they imply? Again the ambiguity is crucial. To dodge it and opt for either reading is to risk missing the point. We do Beckett's texts an injustice, and impoverish them, if we make them more or less agnostic than they are: at the end of the trilogy, the contradictions which fissure *Molloy* are still active.

And yet a case can I think be made for saying that by the attrition to which it subjects the issues at stake throughout the trilogy, *L'Innommable*, for all its austere beauty and rigour, tends to offer these issues a schematic formulation which is more easily assimilable to essentially Romantic perspectives than is the case in *Molloy*. The pathos of selfhood lost or won is arguably too patent in the later text, while the representations which threaten to usurp the subject's claim to integrity lack substance. The endless piping plangency of the unnameable narrator's 'voice', the stark, brutal image of Mahood in his jar, magnificently achieved as they are, tend perhaps to give back to myth what had, in earlier texts, been painstakingly prized from its grip. Moreover, in some ways *L'Innommable* has since it publication come to seem in collusion rather than in collision with some of our modern delineations of selfhood — the version of the subject's tribulations with the word we find in Lacan for example — which are mythic to the extent that they can be identified as being at large in the discourses of our culture. The collusion may be fortuitous and *a posteriori* but the very fact that it is possible marks a contrast with the first novel of Beckett's trilogy. In *Molloy*, the whole currency of our self-images, from the small change of cultural reference to the larger denominations — psychoanalysis, myth, philosophy — is subject to the inflationary spirals and abrupt devaluations that are an inevitable concomitant of its narrative economy. *Molloy* is a more hybrid, plural and unstable book than its immediate successors, and moreover it encompasses their divergent orientations: the desire to lose oneself in stories and the desire to abolish them, the first engendering the narratives and their panoply of discursive threads, the second bathing both narrative and discourse in the vitriol of negation, travesty and ferocious comedy. In surprisingly wide-ranging and subtle ways *Molloy* gives testimony and scope to our inveterate desire for myths and, more generally, coherence; but the novel's remarkable organisation ensures that the realisation of such desires is neither accomplished nor wholly thwarted, but apparently endlessly deferred.

Select Bibliography

I EDITIONS OF 'MOLLOY'

1. *Molloy*, Paris: Edns de Minuit, 1951.
2. *Molloy*, Paris: Edns de Minuit, Collection 'Double', 1982.
3. *Molloy*, Paris: Olympia Press, 1955. [English translation by Patrick Bowles in collaboration with the author.]

II OTHER TEXTS BY BECKETT TO WHICH REFERENCE IS MADE

4. 'Dante ... Bruno, Vico ... Joyce', in *Our Exagmination round his Factification for Incamination of Work in Progress*, London: Faber, 1972.
5. *Proust and Three Dialogues*, London: Calder, 1966.
6. *Murphy*, London: Routledge and Kegan Paul, 1938.
7. *Watt*, Paris: Olympia Press, 1953.
8. *Malone meurt*, Paris: Edns de Minuit, 1953.
9. *L'Innommable*, Paris: Edns de Minuit, 1953.
10. *Nouvelles et textes pour rien*, Paris: Edns de Minuit, 1955.

III CRITICAL WORKS ON 'MOLLOY' AND BECKETT'S TRILOGY

11. Bataille, Georges, 'Le Silence de Molloy', *Critique*, 7 (15 May 1951), 387-96.
12. Bernal, Olga, *Langage et fiction dans le roman de Beckett*, Paris: Gallimard, 1969.
13. Boulais, Véronique, 'Samuel Beckett: une écriture en mal de je', *Poétique*, 17 (1974), 114-32.
14. Fitch, Brian, T., *Dimensions, structures et textualité dans la trilogie romanesque de Beckett*, Paris: Minard, Lettres Modernes, 1977.
15. Fletcher, John, *The Novels of Samuel Beckett*, 2nd edn, London: Chatto and Windus, 1972.
16. ——, 'Interpreting *Molloy*' in *30*, 107-93.
17. Janvier, Ludovic, *Pour Samuel Beckett*, Paris: Edns de Minuit, 1966.
18. Mooney, Michael E., 'Molloy, part 1: Beckett's 'Discourse on Method'', *Journal of Beckett Studies*, 3, (1980), 40-55.
19. Moorjani, Angela B., 'A Mythic Reading of *Molloy*' in *33*, pp.47-89.
20. Morot-Sir, E., 'Samuel Beckett and Cartesian Emblems' in *33*, pp.21-49.
21. Mayoux, Jean-Jacques, '*Molloy*: un événement littéraire, une œuvre', (Afterword to *2*, pp.243-74).

22. O'Hara, J.D., 'Jung and the Narratives of *Molloy*', *Journal of Beckett Studies*, 7 (1982), 19-48.
23. Rabinovitz, Rubin, "*Molloy*' and the archetypal Traveller', *Journal of Beckett Studies*, 5 (Autumn 1979), 25-44.
24. Rolin-Janziti, J., 'Le Système générateur dans *Molloy* de Samuel Beckett', *Lingua et Stile*, 16 (1981), 255-70.
25. Saint-Martin, Fernande, *Samuel Beckett et l'univers de la fiction*, Montreal: University Press, 1976.
26. Scherzer, Dina, *Structure de la trilogie de Beckett: 'Molloy', 'Malone meurt', 'L'Innommable'*, The Hague, Paris: Mouton, 1976.
27. Solomon, Philip H., *The Life after Birth: Imagery in Samuel Beckett's Trilogy*, Mississippi University Romance Monographs, 1975.

IV GENERAL CRITICISM ON BECKETT

28. Bair, Deirdre, *Samuel Beckett*, London, Jonathan Cape, 1978.
29. Graver, Lawrence and Raymond Federman, *Samuel Beckett: the Critical Heritage*, London: Routledge and Kegan Paul, 1979.
30. Friedman, Melvin J., *Samuel Beckett Now*, Chicago: University Press, 2nd edn, 1975.
31. Kenner, Hugh, *Samuel Beckett*, London: Calder and Boyars, 1966.
32. Morot-Sir, E., H. Harper and D. McMillan (eds), *Samuel Beckett: the Art of Rhetoric*, Chapel Hill: North Carolina University Press, 1976.
33. O'Hara, J.D., *Twentieth Century Interpretations of 'Molloy', 'Malone dies', 'The Unnamable'*, New Jersey: Prentice Hall, 1970.
34. Pilling, John, *Samuel Beckett*, London: Routledge and Kegan Paul, 1976.

V GENERAL WORKS

35. Cohn, Dorrit, *Transparent Minds*, Princeton: University Press, 1978.
36. Chatman, Seymour, *Story and Discourse*, Cornell: University Press, 1978.
37. Genette, Gérard, *Figures III*, Paris: Edns du Seuil, 1973.
38. Jefferson, Ann, *The Nouveau Roman and the Poetics of Fiction*, Cambridge: University Press, 1980.
39. Ricardou, Jean, *Problèmes du nouveau roman*, Paris: Edns du Seuil, 1972.

CRITICAL GUIDES TO FRENCH TEXTS

edited by

Roger Little, Wolfgang van Emden, David Williams